RAND

A New Methodology for Assessing Multilayer Missile Defense Options

Eric V. Larson, Glenn A. Kent

Prepared for the
United States Air Force

Project AIR FORCE

Preface

This report describes a methodology for determining the optimal allocation of resources to multilayer theater missile defenses, and it is an aid for thinking about theater missile defenses based upon the methodology. The work supporting the report was conducted under the Force Modernization and Employment program of Project AIR FORCE. The research was undertaken in support of the 1993 USAF Scientific Advisory Board summer study investigating theater missile defense investment strategies. This report should be of interest to those responsible for defining or assessing operational concepts, policymakers, program analysts, budgeters, and others who are involved in making decisions about missile defense programs. It also should be of interest to operations researchers, systems analysts, modelers, and others with an interest in mathematical approaches to solving complex defense problems.

Project AIR FORCE

Project AIR FORCE, a division of RAND, is the Air Force federally funded research and development center (FFRDC) for studies and analyses. It provides the Air Force with independent analyses of policy alternatives affecting the development, employment, combat readiness, and support of current and future aerospace forces. Research is carried out in three programs: Strategy, Doctrine, and Force Structure; Force Modernization and Employment; and Resource Management and System Acquisition.

Project AIR FORCE is operated under Contract F49620-91-C-0003 between the Air Force and RAND.

Brent Bradley is Vice President and Director of Project AIR FORCE. Those interested in further information concerning Project AIR FORCE should contact his office directly:

Brent D. Bradley
RAND
1700 Main Street
P.O. Box 2138
Santa Monica, California 90407-2138

Contents

Figures

Tables

Summary

Iraqi Scud missile attacks during the Persian Gulf War dramatized U.S. vulnerability to theater ballistic (and potentially, cruise) missiles and illustrated all too clearly the threat of large-scale casualties to U.S. and allied forces posed by proliferating weapons of mass destruction around the world. The presence of these weapons could serve as a strong deterrent on U.S. actions, and could even result in constraining U.S. forces from achieving their objectives in regional conflicts.

In light of these threats, U.S. planning for theater missile defense has shifted. In contrast to missile defense in the Cold War era, future missile defense operations are envisaged as part of a theater-level and essentially conventional campaign against adversaries with relatively small missile arsenals.

This research focuses on one part of U.S. theater ballistic missile defense: active defense operations that destroy missiles after launch over the course of a campaign. We set out to determine how to allocate increasingly scarce resources among the various "pillars" of missile defense. More specifically, the question we posed was: How can we determine the optimum allocation of resources—where optimum means achieving a demanded probability that no attacking objects will survive all the layers of a missile defense and arrive intact at the intended target—at least cost? This report describes a methodology for making such allocations. It also attempts to illuminate the relationship between outcomes and resources in order to clarify where the greatest leverage for cost-effective investment lies.

Approach

Our discussion of methodology for resource allocation begins simply and becomes increasingly complex:

- First, we describe the overall logic of the methodology by using a simple worksheet-based approach (Section 2).

- Then we describe the principal cost drivers of missile defense: layering, the size of the attacker's missile inventory, the demanded probability of no survivors, and the effectiveness of interceptors in each layer. We also consider several operational parameters (i.e., fractionation, saturation and exhaustion, and multiple sites to provide a "footprint") and cost variations (i.e., different interceptor costs among layers and buy-in costs). Using our basic model we are able to demonstrate how these factors affect the optimal allocation (Sections 3–5).

- Next, we examine the effect of some critical uncertainties on the size of the missile defense system and demonstrate how much the inventory needs to be augmented to maintain confidence that the interceptors will not be exhausted before the campaign is over (Section 6).

- Finally, we provide an illustrative mission area analysis to show how the model might be used to assess broad programmatic tradeoffs within a mission area (Section 7).

Worksheet-Based Method

The expected-value methodology defines the total resources the defender must expend in order to deploy a defense that achieves the demanded probability of no survivors over the campaign against a defined threat. The total resources are measured in terms of the number of interceptors the defense must deploy per object in the attacker's inventory. The principal value of the worksheet approach is that it uses a relatively simple parametric formulation for quantifying—in a simplified analytic setting—the optimal allocation of resources to various layers in a multilayered defense.

The table below demonstrates an illustrative worksheet for determining the least-cost allocation of resources to a three-layer theater missile defense.[1] The table shows the case where the single-shot probability of kill (*SSPk*) in each layer is 1/2 and costs are treated in terms of the required interceptor inventory. We assume a demand for eight engagements per attacking object in the third layer. In other words, the problem is initially structured so that the number of engagements per attacking object in the last layer is specified and the optimal allocation in the previous layers is determined. This simple formulation is later discarded in favor of a less restrictive one.

We gain several insights from the worksheet:

- With no interceptors in the first and second layer (row one of the table), the "cost" is, by definition, eight interceptors per attacking object.

---

[1]We consider the term "layer" to be synonymous with a separate "look-shoot" and not necessarily tied to the conventional association with separate phases of missile defense (such as prelaunch, boost, postboost, midcourse, and terminal).

Table S.1

Worksheet for Determining the Least-Cost Defense Allocation

Layer									Total E/SO	Total Cost/IO
1st			2nd			3rd				
f	E/PO	c	f	E/PO	c	f	E/PO	c		
			1	0	1·0=0	1	8	1·8=8	8	8
			1	1	1	1/2	8	4	9	5
			1	2	2	1/4	8	2	10	4
			1	**3**	**3**	**1/8**	**8**	**1**	**11**	**4**
			1	4	4	1/16	8	1/2	12	4 1/2
1	0	0	1	3	3	1/8	8	1	11	4
1	1	1	1/2	3	3/2	1/16	8	1/2	12	3
1	**2**	**2**	**1/4**	**3**	**3/4**	**1/32**	**8**	**1/4**	**13**	**3**
1	3	3	1/8	3	3/8	1/64	8	1/8	14	3 1/2

NOTE: $SSPk = 1/2$, one cost unit per assigned interceptor, for all layers. Preferred allocations in bold. f is the fraction of the initial attacking force leaking to that layer. c is the cost per interceptor, assumed to be identical (1) for all layers. E/PO is the number of engagements per presented object, and Total E/SO is the total number of engagements per surviving object. Total Cost/IO is the expected total cost per inventory object. The probability of no survivors varies from .77 (with 8 total engagements per surviving object) to .99 (with 14 total engagements per surviving object).

- If we deploy (and fire) one interceptor per object in the second layer, then the total cost is five interceptors per attacking object: we must deploy one interceptor per object in the second layer, which halves the third layer's original cost of eight to four, since only half of the objects are expected to penetrate to the third layer.

- With either two or three engagements per object in the second layer (but still none in the first), the total "cost" is reduced to four—a total of four interceptors must be deployed per attacking object. We prefer three intercepts to two in the second layer because it gives a total of 11 (instead of 10) intercepts per object at the same cost of four.

- Four engagements per object in the second layer reduces the fraction seen by the last layer to 1/16, but such allocation also increases the expected total cost to 4 1/2, so it is not optimal.

- The bottom half of the worksheet shows that resources can be optimized for all three layers by changing the first layer. If, for example, we deploy two interceptors per object in the first layer, we can further reduce the total cost to three interceptors per attacking object. That is, three interceptors per attacking object must be deployed to meet the stated demand of eight engagements per object in the third layer at least cost. This results in a total of 13 engagements per surviving object—two in the first layer, three in the second, and eight in the third. Again, we see more engagements per surviving object at lower cost.

We conclude, then, that the optimal firing doctrine, when eight engagements are demanded in the last layer, is two per warhead in the first layer, three in the second layer, and eight in the last layer.

Principal Cost Drivers

Layering and Size of Attacker's Inventory

The size of the interceptor inventory necessary to achieve a demanded probability of no survivors is highly sensitive to the existence of multiple look-shoots or layers. All other things being equal, the more the layers, the greater the reduction in inventory, and therefore cost.

Figure S.1 shows the ratio of the expected number of interceptors to the attack size, assuming that the probability of no survivors is held at greater than 90 percent. As the figure shows, both the two- and three-layer systems require far fewer interceptors per attacking object than the single-layer system to achieve the desired outcome. And the ratio is quite insensitive to the total number of attacking objects. Increasing this number by a factor of 16 (from 256 to 4096 attacking missiles) increases the ratio from 2.97 to only 3.09.

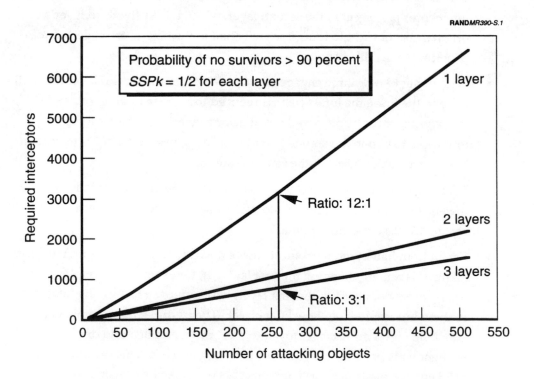

Figure S.1—Layering Reduces Sensitivity to Attack Size

Demanding a Higher Probability of No Survivors

With a multilayered defense, tightening the demand for no survivors can be achieved at a relatively small increase in total system cost. Take, for example, the case of 64 attacking objects against a defense having interceptors with *SSPk* of 1/2, as shown in Table S.2.

To attain a probability of success above zero in the second significant figure (i.e., .02) requires a total of four engagements per surviving object (i.e., any object that survives will have incurred a total of four engagements). In turn, the demand for four total engagements per surviving object requires that 2.0 interceptors be deployed per inventory object. A demand for a probability of no survivors of 94 percent requires 10 engagements per surviving object—an increase of a factor of 2.5 in terms of total engagements (10 divided by 4). However, as the table shows, the cost is increased to only 2.85—a factor of 1.425 (or 2.85 divided by 2).

Increasing Interceptor Effectiveness

Interceptor effectiveness, on the other hand, has a significant effect on overall inventory requirements and costs. For example, if the interceptor effectiveness or *SSPk* increases from 1/2 to 3/4 and all other factors are held constant, the demand on total deployed resources is reduced by a factor of two, because it takes two intercepts of .5 to have the same effectiveness as one interceptor of .75. On the other hand, if the *SSPk* degrades from .5 to .29, then the average demand on resources doubles: it takes two interceptors with *SSPk* of .29 to equal the effectiveness of one interceptor with *SSPk* of .5. Since we claim no knowledge of

Table S.2

**Engagements per Surviving Object, Probability of
No Survivors, and Total Cost per Attacker's
Inventory Object for an Optimized
Three-Layer Defense**

E/SO	Probability of No Survivors	Total Cost/IO
4	.02	2.00
6	.37	2.38
8	.78	2.63
10	.94	2.85

NOTE: E/SO is total engagements incurred by any surviving object. Total Cost/IO is the total cost per attacker's inventory object.

the actual *SSPk* that interceptors may attain in battle, we assume an *SSPk* of 1/2. The methodology, being parametric, readily handles other values.

Operational Cost Drivers

This methodology can also accommodate operational factors, such as fractionation and multiple terminal defense sites, which affect the overall cost of a missile defense system. We quantitatively demonstrate that fractionation—the dispensing of submunitions or multiple warheads—can severely burden even a layered defense. Our analysis shows that an optimized layered defense should shift resources to the first layer, or "prefractionation," defense units because of the leverage provided by early intercept—and the cost of fielding systems to defend against the expanded number of attacking objects after fractionation.

The analysis shows the effect on allocation and cost when multiple terminal defense sites are required in the last layer to adequately defend a designated "footprint." As in the case of fractionation, it is more effective to allocate interceptors in layers prior to terminal defenses; costs per inventory object also increase.[2]

Hedging Against Uncertainties

Clearly, there are limitations in using expected values to determine the number of interceptors to deploy for a particular campaign. Expected values are only a surrogate for probability distributions; the actual number of kills in a given defense layer will depend on the "luck of the draw." Therefore, we need to hedge against randomness: we must determine the inventory size that gives us confidence that all the interceptors will not be exhausted before the campaign is over.

The parametric expected-value approach documented in this report lends itself nicely to simulation techniques that can be used to estimate the inventory size needed to provide such confidence. We used Monte Carlo techniques to explore the distribution of the number of interceptors needed to provide 90 percent probability that in any particular campaign none of the layers would run out of interceptors. For example, the simulation of 100 campaigns against 64 attackers suggested that a 20 percent increase in interceptors over the average number is required to achieve that level of confidence.

---

[2]See Table 4.2.

Mission Area Analysis

We demonstrated how the methodology can be used to generate a "mission area analysis" or COEA (cost and operational effectiveness analysis) for theater missile defense that compared different programmatic options in terms of effectiveness, marginal costs, and buy-in costs. Using notional numbers for the cost of the options, we demonstrated the richness and relevance of such a framework in defining overall investment strategy in this mission area.

Concluding Remarks

Our main purpose in this research was to define a methodology for determining how to allocate resources among layers of a multilayered missile defense—a methodology that was simple in its logic but versatile enough to address complex planning considerations. In the process of this analysis, certain broad policy implications for future investment strategy became clear:

- There are many benefits inherent in a multilayered architecture for missile defense.

- The costs of such an architecture are substantial. However, a high level of effectiveness is achievable at far lower cost with multiple layers than with only a single layer.

- There is great leverage in engaging attacking objects at the earliest possible stage. Because intercepts after fractionation are so difficult to accomplish and so costly, it is more desirable to intercept before fractionation.

Historically, however, the emphasis in missile defenses has been focused on the terminal layer, where, our methodology shows, the leverage does not exist. But it does more than that—it quantifies in a simple parametric model the major factors that must be considered in designing an optimal multilayer missile defense.

Acknowledgments

The authors wish to thank a number of individuals who have provided their support, ideas, and reactions to our work at various stages of development.

We wish to thank Natalie Crawford of RAND, who chaired the 1993 United States Air Force Scientific Advisory Board (SAB) summer study on theater missile defenses, and Dr. Robert Selden, Los Alamos National Laboratory, who chaired the panel of the SAB in which the authors participated. Within RAND, we wish to thank Ted Harshberger and Bart Bennett, associate program directors within Project AIR FORCE, for providing support for this effort, and Dick Hillestad for his willingness to free up one of the authors from other project responsibilities while performing this research. Also within RAND, we wish to especially thank Michael Miller, but also David Vaughan and Dean Wilkening for the many suggestions, ideas, and proofs they offered; Rich Mesic and Russ Shaver for their additional suggestions and comments; and Paul Davis, Keith Henry, Tom Lucas, and Irving Lachow for their comments on earlier drafts. Thanks also to Laura Zakaras and Nikki Shacklett for their editorial assistance. For their comments on earlier drafts of this document, we wish to thank Maj Gen Donald L. Lamberson, USAF (Ret.), Maj Gen Jasper Welch, USAF (Ret.), Col Robert Gibson, United States Air Force Studies and Analysis, Col Chris Waln, AFPEO/SP, and Fred Nyland.

1. Introduction

The Iraqi use of Scud ballistic missiles in the 1991 Persian Gulf War dramatized the vulnerability of U.S. forces and in-theater infrastructure to theater ballistic (and cruise) missiles, and the grave threat that such weapons can pose to U.S. forces deploying to future major and lesser regional contingencies. The Soviet threat that was the impetus for many earlier U.S. investments in missile defenses has been replaced by a new operational environment, with a somewhat different set of constraints and considerations:

- Missile defense operations are currently envisaged as part of a theater-level and essentially conventional campaign against adversaries who may have ballistic and cruise missiles.

- Nevertheless, the threat of large-scale casualties caused by ballistic and cruise missiles—made possible by proliferating weapons of mass destruction (WMD)—could serve as a strong deterrent or constraint on U.S. actions, or even result in pressures for constraining U.S. forces before they achieve operational or strategic objectives.

- For the foreseeable future, the likely size of missile arsenals held by potential adversaries—and the size of the barrages those adversaries will be able to generate—will remain orders of magnitude smaller than the size of the Soviet ballistic missile arsenal that shaped missile defense planning in the past. This makes it possible to plan defenses against somewhat smaller and more limited threats.

- Current U.S. conventional campaign planning envisages gaining air superiority (and supremacy) over enemy airspace, enabling attacks against ballistic missile facilities and supporting infrastructure. By contrast, air superiority over the Soviet Union was not a realistic objective, a fact that greatly constrained or denied any opportunity for prelaunch, preburnout and prefractionation intercepts.

- Past planning was somewhat more oriented toward midcourse/terminal defenses programmed under less austere budgets. For example, the U.S. Navy's AEGIS system was originally envisaged as providing midcourse and terminal defense primarily for Navy battle groups (and possibly ports), and the U.S. Army's Patriot system, for providing midcourse and terminal defense (primarily for deployed Army forces, air bases and ports, and population centers). By contrast, the current milieu places a premium on joint operations, synergism between the missile defense capabilities of various missile defense "pillars" (prelaunch, boost phase, midcourse, and terminal), and cost-effectiveness.

These differences in the presumed operational and budgetary environments suggest that it is time to raise the following question: How should we think about the problem of allocating increasingly scarce resources among the various "pillars" of missile defense so that we can understand where the leverage is? This report describes an expected-value methodology for explicitly determining the optimal (least-cost) allocation of resources to various layers of a multilayer missile defense to counter theater ballistic missiles in a simplified analytic setting. The methodology also provides a means of illuminating the relationship between demanded outcomes and total resources that must be deployed to achieve those outcomes. The approach is offered as a starting point, an initial attempt to create a broader framework for evaluating the contributions of various operational concepts and force elements in countering theater ballistic missiles. The calculus is offered in the hope that additional work by others will help to clarify further the proper mix of resources among the various force elements attendant to this mission.

Caveats

We now wish to offer several caveats about the mathematical model we present. First, we have no illusions that the expected values we report will hold in any particular campaign. Generally, our calculus is based on a requirement of greater than 90 percent probability of success; if a person really believed the expected values that were mathematically derived would hold in a particular campaign, he should be willing to give nine-to-one odds that in an actual campaign no attacking objects will survive. The authors would give no such odds, however, because in addition to the uncertainties we assess, there are other operational factors that may further degrade expected results:

- There are likely to be gaps in engaging objects, especially in the context of a stressful environment, where some objects may not receive the required number of engagements.

- There will be correlated errors in kill assessment and engagement. For example, some objects will not be engaged because they are not seen at all—and correlated error could occur both within and even among layers. Furthermore, the "probability of a hit given an engagement" is not apt to be independent among the shots in a salvo, as an object "hit but not killed" by one interceptor may be a much tougher target for the next interceptor to kill. That is, the "kill given a hit" may be substantially reduced for objects that have been previously "hit" but not killed.

Despite these misgivings about actual campaign outcomes, we believe the methodology to be quite useful in providing a way of thinking about the total concept of an optimized multilayered defense, in gaining insights regarding the allocation of resources in various layers, and in illuminating the total resources the defender must expend for any kind of a robust and effective theater defense. Furthermore, many of these degradation effects might be adequately captured by adjusting the values of parameters used in the model to conform with off-line analyses, or by adding new parameters, without compromising the elegance of the basic methodology.

Organization of the Report

This document is organized to present an approach to optimally allocating resources for multilayered missile defenses.

- We begin in Section 2 by describing a simple parametric approach to determining how to optimally allocate resources among layers of a multilayer missile defense system.

- In Section 3, we identify the principal cost drivers of missile defense and discuss how these factors affect the optimal allocation of resources. We present a number of excursions to show how the number of layers, size of the attacker's inventory, demanded probability of no survivors of an attacking force, and the likely effectiveness of interceptors in each layer affect the optimal allocation of resources.

- In Section 4, we examine four operational factors that drive the optimal allocation of resources to missile defenses: the quality of kill assessment, fractionation, saturation and exhaustion, and multiple terminal sites to provide a "footprint."

- In Section 5, we examine the impact of two cost-related considerations on the optimal allocation: interceptor costs and buy-in costs.

- In Section 6 we provide an illustrative mission area analysis, also known as a "mission area COEA" (cost and operational effectiveness analysis). The focus is on demonstrating an approach for assessing macro-level programmatic options within a mission area.

4

- In Section 7, we show how uncertainty affects the size of the inventory of interceptors necessary to hedge against critical uncertainties.

- In Section 8, we provide concluding remarks.

2. Determining the Optimal Allocation of Resources

What Should Be Optimized?

There is general agreement that a critical measure of outcome for theater missile defenses is the probability that none of an inventory of attacking warheads survives the missile defense system—"the probability of no survivors."[1] This probability extends over the duration of the campaign—not just a single attack. This has the benefit of being both operationally oriented and providing a clear criterion for assessing the relative merits of different operational and system concepts.

The first purpose of this report is to provide basic insights into how to determine the optimal allocation of resources across the layers of theater missile defense—optimal in the sense of achieving a given measure of outcome (i.e., a stated probability of no survivors of an attacking force) at least cost. This section demonstrates a simplified version of the parametric expected-value approach for determining such an allocation.

Definitions

We begin by defining some key terms:

- We consider the term "layer" to be synonymous with a separate "look-shoot," and not necessarily tied to the conventional association with separate phases of missile defense (e.g., prelaunch, boost, postboost, midcourse, and terminal). One implication of this is that there needn't be a single "look-shoot" in each phase; multiple "look-shoots" may (and as we will see, perhaps should) take place within a particular phase.

- The single-shot "probability of kill" (*SSPk*) is defined as the conditional probability that an object will be killed, given an engagement by a single interceptor.

---

[1]This is similar to one of several effectiveness criteria discussed in A. Ross Eckler and Stefan A. Burr, *Mathematical Models of Target Coverage and Missile Allocations*, Alexandria, VA: Military Operations Research Society, 1972, pp. 3–6, and in Ashton B. Carter, "BMD Applications: Performance and Limitations," in Ashton B. Carter and David N. Schwartz (eds.), *Ballistic Missile Defense*, Washington, D.C.: The Brookings Institution, 1984, pp. 98–181 and especially pp. 99–105.

- We use the term "interceptor" to connote a defending system available to engage an attacking object.

- We will use the term "engagement" as meaning a single interceptor fired against a single attacking object.

- "Engagements per presented object" (E/PO) is the number of engagements an object incurs in a layer if it reaches that layer.

- "Total engagements per surviving object" (Total E/SO) is the total number of engagements that would have been incurred by any object that leaked through the entire system.

- "Cost per inventory object" (Cost/IO) is the expected total cost in interceptors that would be fired at each of an inventory of attacking objects.

Finding the Optimal Allocation of Resources

Table 2.1 presents an illustrative worksheet for allocating resources to a three-layer theater missile defense.[2]

Table 2.1

Worksheet for Determining the Least-Cost Defense Allocation

				Layer					Total	Total
	1st			2nd			3rd		E/SO	Cost/IO
f	E/PO	c	f	E/PO	c	f	E/PO	c		
			1	0	$1{\cdot}0=0$	1	8	$1{\cdot}8=8$	8	8
			1	1	1	1/2	8	4	9	5
			1	2	2	1/4	8	2	10	4
			1	**3**	**3**	**1/8**	**8**	**1**	**11**	**4**
			1	4	4	1/16	8	1/2	12	4 1/2
1	0	0	1	3	3	1/8	8	1	11	4
1	1	1	1/2	3	3/2	1/16	8	1/2	12	3
1	**2**	**2**	**1/4**	**3**	**3/4**	**1/32**	**8**	**1/4**	**13**	**3**
1	3	3	1/8	3	3/8	1/64	8	1/8	14	3 1/2

NOTE: $SSPk = 1/2$, one cost unit per assigned interceptor, for all layers. Preferred allocations in bold. f is the fraction of the initial attacking force leaking to that layer. c is the cost per interceptor, assumed to be identical (1) for all layers. E/PO is the number of engagements per presented object, and Total E/SO is the total number of engagements per surviving object. Total Cost/IO is the expected total cost per inventory object.

The probability of no survivors varies from .77 (with 8 total engagements per surviving object) to .99 (with 14 total engagements per surviving object).

---

[2]For many of the examples used in this report, parameter values (e.g., $SSPk$ of 1/2) have been chosen to illustrate a concept and point the reader's thinking in the right direction. Computations and derivation of more general "rules" for cases with other parameter values would likely be somewhat messier.

The table portrays the case where the single-shot probability of kill (*SSPk*) in each layer is 1/2, and costs are treated in terms of the required interceptor inventory.[3] We assume, for this example, a demand that there be eight engagements per attacking object in the last (third) layer. That is, for illustrative purposes, the problem is initially structured such that the number of engagements per attacking object desired in the last layer is specified, and the optimal allocation in the previous layers is determined. This most simple formulation will later be discarded in favor of a less restrictive one.

The worksheet has three columns for each layer. The first column, designated "*f*," is the fraction of the initial attack that penetrates to that layer. The second column, designated "E/PO," is the number of engagements incurred by each object (missile or warhead) presented to that layer. And the third column, "*c*," is the computed deployment cost per attacker's inventory object for that layer—this being the product of the fraction of the attack seen by that layer and the number of engagements incurred by the object in that layer.[4] The column titled "Total E/SO" totals the number of engagements incurred by any attacking object that survives through the last layer, and represents the sum of the E/POs for the three layers. The "Total Cost/IO" is the total cost per inventory object—the sum of the costs for the three individual layers, and represents the expected total number of interceptors the defender must deploy for each object the attacker presents to the defense over the campaign.

Optimizing Among the Last Two Layers

Let us first consider several of the possible allocations of interceptors to the second layer when the last layer is fixed at eight engagements per surviving object. As shown in Table 2.1:

- If no interceptors are assigned in the first or second layers (row one of the table), the expected cost remains eight, because the third layer sees the entirety of the attack.

- If there is no allocation in layer one, and just one engagement per presented object is allocated to the second layer, the cost is one in that layer, since it sees the entire attack. Because only $1/2^1 = 1/2$ of the attack reaches the third

---

[3]In the interests of simplicity of presentation, we initially assume equal *SSPk* and per-engagement costs in all layers, and perfect kill assessment. The required interceptor inventory will be used initially as a surrogate for cost; we will later impute a relationship between interceptors and dollars, so that programmatic and budgetary costs may be considered more explicitly.

[4]With an equal cost of one unit per interceptor for all layers, the number of interceptors used is identical to the inventory cost.

layer, the cost for that layer is halved, for a third-layer cost of four. Thus, the expected total cost per inventory object drops from eight to five, while the total number of engagements per surviving object rises from eight to nine.

- If two engagements per object are allocated to the second layer, the third layer sees $1/2^2 = 1/4$ of the attack, resulting in an expected 10 engagements per surviving object at an average total cost per inventory object of just four. Again, we see more engagements per surviving object at lower cost.

- However, if three interceptors per object are bought for the second layer, $1/2^3 = 1/8$ of the initial attackers penetrate to the last layer, and the missile defense system can realize 11 engagements per object for that same cost of four. Since we get one more engagement per surviving object (i.e., it yields a higher probability of no survivors) at the same expected total cost, we prefer this allocation to only two engagements per object in the second layer.[5]

- Four engagements per object in the second layer reduces the fraction seen by the last layer to $1/2^4 = 1/16$, but it increases the expected total cost to 4 1/2. Thus we see that we are moving away from the optimal least-cost allocation by going beyond three engagements per presented object in the second layer.

Optimizing for All Three Layers by Changing the First Layer

Similarly, in the bottom half of the worksheet, we determine the optimal number of engagements per object for the first layer of the three-layer missile defense system, given the already optimized two-layer system, consisting of the second and third layers. As can be seen:

- We begin with the optimal allocation for the second and third layers we just considered, repeated in the first line of the three-layer system: no engagements in the first layer, for an expected total cost of four per inventory object.

- If we provide one engagement per object in the first layer, the second layer sees only 1/2 of the initial attacking force and the expected total cost falls from four to three per object. Note now that there are 12 total engagements. Again, we see more engagements per object at lower cost.

---

[5]Although we will not describe it further, there is an important recursion in evidence here: for cases where the *SSPk* is 1/2, the optimal number of engagements per object in the second layer is the log to the base two of the number in the last layer. Furthermore, while not proved here, it can be shown that by fixing the probability of no survivors and leaving the total inventory of interceptors unconstrained, our expected-value methodology produces estimates of the expected number of interceptors expended that are identical to those generated using the exact binomial expansion. That is, the simplified framework we offer does not sacrifice accuracy.

- If we provide two engagements per object, 1/4 of the initial attack survives to the second layer, and we can get a total of 13 engagements per object for the same cost of three. Since we can get one more engagement at no additional cost, we prefer this solution to only one engagement in the first layer.

- If we were to provide three engagements per attacking object in the first layer, the expected total cost would rise from three to 3 1/2 units. Hence, two engagements per object in the first layer is the optimum solution.

We conclude, then, that the optimal firing doctrine, when eight engagements are demanded in the last layer, is two engagements per warhead in the first layer, three engagements per warhead in the second layer, and by assumption, the demanded eight engagements in the last layer, for a total of 13 engagements per surviving object. In the course of achieving the least-cost allocation, we encountered a somewhat striking and counterintuitive phenomenon: as we approached the optimal allocation, the number of engagements for each surviving object (a measure of the effectiveness of the missile defense system) rose, while the expected cost per attacking warhead decreased.

We can mathematically show that the function for cost per attacking object is convex and has a unique minimum point, as can be seen in Figures 2.1 and 2.2, which portray the cost per attacking object as a function of the number of engagements per object in the first layer. Figure 2.1 is for the two-layer case described above in which the second layer is fixed at eight engagements per object, and Figure 2.2 is for the three-layer case in which the second layer is fixed at three and the last layer is fixed at eight engagements per object.[6]

Recursion in the Optimal Allocation

Having described a procedure for optimally allocating resources when the last layer is fixed,[7] we will now drop this formulation and show how to determine the optimal allocation of a fixed number of engagements per attacking object. Consider Table 2.2, which portrays an interesting recursion in the optimal

---

[6]The function that is being graphed in Figure 2.1 is $x + dq^x$, where d is the integer number of engagements per object demanded in the last layer and x is the integer number of engagements per object in the first layer. The function being graphed in Figure 2.2 is $x + yq^x + dq^{x+y}$, where d is as above, x is engagements per object in layer one, and y is engagements per object in layer two.

[7]The results in this report were either generated or verified with a spreadsheet model implemented in Microsoft Excel that determines the least-cost allocation by performing an exhaustive search of possible allocations while taking into account the number of layers, $SSPk$ and cost of interceptors in each layer, and other key parameters.

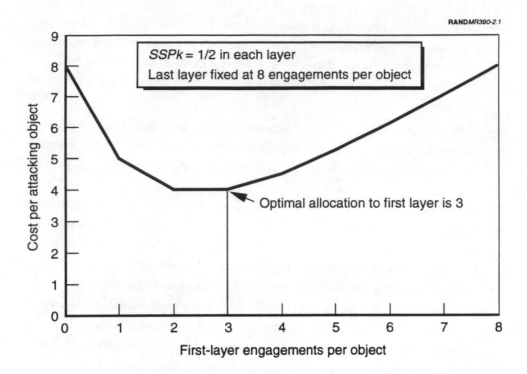

Figure 2.1—Cost Implications of Various Allocations to First Layer, Two-Layer System

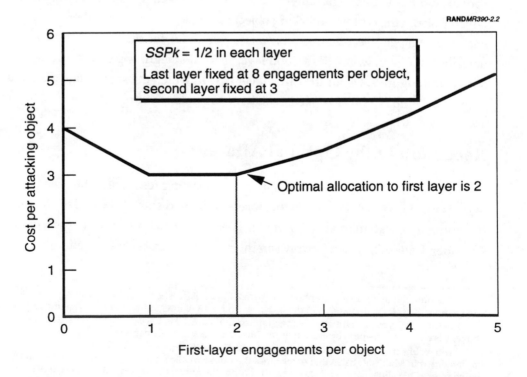

Figure 2.2—Cost Implications of Various Allocations to First Layer, Three-Layer System

Table 2.2

An Illustration of Recursion in the Optimal Allocation

Engagements per Presented Object				
1st Layer	2nd Layer	3rd Layer	Total E/SO	Total Cost/IO
0	0	1	1	1.00
1	1	2	4	2.00
1	2	4	7	2.50
2	3	8	13	3.00
2	4	16	22	3.25
2	5	32	39	3.50
2	6	64	72	3.75
3	7	128	138	4.00

NOTE: $SSPk = 1/2$, one cost unit per assigned interceptor, for all layers. Total E/PO is total engagements per presented object. Total Cost/IO is the expected total cost in interceptors for each of the attacker's inventory of attacking objects.

allocation of resources to three-layer missile defenses for various demanded numbers of total engagements per object.[8]

As can be seen from the table:

- There is a clear mathematical relationship among the number of engagements in the three layers for those "canonical cases" in which the third-layer allocation is a power of two: the number of engagements per surviving warhead in the second layer is the log to the base two of the number in the third layer,[9] and the number of engagements in the first layer is the integer part of the log to the base two of one plus the number in the second layer.[10]

- As the total number of engagements rises, it can be seen that the cost flattens out.

Some readers may believe that a salvo size of eight or even four engagements per object presented to a layer—or seven or more total engagments per surviving object—is an excessive number of engagements. There are two important points to be made on this matter at this point in our presentation.[11] First of all, if we demand a high confidence of zero leakers, we may have little choice but to use

---

[8]The fourth row, for example, corresponds to the optimal allocation in Table 2.1.

[9]This relationship holds for the case of $SSPk = 1/2$.

[10]Furthermore, we can solve for the number of engagements in the first layer explicitly. Let x be the number of engagements per object in the first layer, y be the number of engagements in the remaining layers, and q be $1 - SSPk$. We desire to minimize $x + y \cdot q^x$. Taking the first derivative and setting it to zero, we get $1 + y \cdot q^x \cdot \ln(q) = 0$. Rearranging, we find that $x = (1 / \ln(q)) \cdot \ln(-1/(y \cdot \ln(q)))$. Since the function is convex, the optimal integer solution is an immediate neighbor of this value.

[11]Later we will talk about a third: the effect of uncertainty.

12

salvos to achieve that level of confidence. Second, the methodology is in fact parametric, and it is for illustrative and pedagogical reasons that we have generally assumed a relatively modest *SSPk* of 1/2 for interceptors. As we will later show, more effective interceptors can substantially reduce the total number of engagements per surviving object required to achieve a demanded level of confidence of zero leakers.

Having described some of the characteristics of an optimized multilayer missile defense, we will now restate the problem in two ways that are more relevant in an operational context: (1) determining the least-cost firing doctrine and allocation of resources to achieve a demanded outcome (i.e., a demanded probability of no survivors), and (2) determining the optimal firing doctrine (i.e., that yielding the highest probability of no survivors) given a constrained interceptor inventory.

The Optimal Allocation to Achieve a Demanded Outcome

As described in the example of Figure 2.3, the first of these two optimization problems seeks to find the least-cost solution to achieving a demanded probability of no survivors.

Let:

$SSPk$ = 1/2 for all layers,

W = the number of initial attacking warheads = 64,

cost per interceptor = 1 for all layers,

$p_0(W)$ 90 percent, where $p_0(W)$ is the probability of no survivors,

given W.

Fix the number of layers.

Find least-cost allocation to achieve the stated outcome.

Figure 2.3—Achieving a Demanded Level of Outcome

Consider the case of 64 attacking warheads against a three-layer missile defense system, an *SSPk* of 1/2 for each layer,[12] and a demand for greater than 90 percent probability of no survivors.[13] The first step in the problem is to determine how many engagements against each surviving object are required to achieve the >90 percent probability of no survivors.[14] This is shown in Figure 2.4.[15]

In the cases where the *SSPk* for each layer is the same, the demanded probability of no survivors can readily be translated into the total required number of

What is the least integer number *S* of engagements per attacking object

that provides >90 percent for $P_0(W)$ given *W*, where

W = the number of initial attacking warheads = 64,

SSPk = 1/2 for all layers?

$P_0(W) = [1 - (1 - SSPk)^S]^W$ = the probability of no survivors.

By solving for *S* analytically, we find that *S* = 9.2.

Since we want an integral number of engagements per surviving

warhead, we take the first integer larger than 9.2, or *S* = 10.

Figure 2.4—Probability of No Survivors and Required Engagements per Object

---

[12]To repeat a point made earlier, *SSPk* is initially asserted to be identical to the single-shot probability that a target does not survive any given engagement.

[13]We have arbitrarily chosen greater than 90 percent probability of no survivors as our criterion for the examples in this report. The methodology is, however, applicable to any desired level of confidence.

[14]The number of engagements against each surviving object represents what the defense wants to ensure it allocates against any object that might leak through.

[15]We can solve analytically using the formula

$$S = \ln(1 - P_0^{1/W})/\ln(1 - SSPk),$$

where

   S = the required number of shots,
   P_0 = the demanded probability of no survivors,
   W = the number of attacking objects, and
   SSPk = the single-shot probability of kill.

engagements against each surviving object of the original attack. In the stylized case portrayed in Figure 2.4, the demand for >90 percent probability of no survivors against 64 warheads translates to a requirement for 10 total engagements of each surviving object (i.e., any warhead that survives all layers of defenses will have incurred 10 engagements).

If all engagements were incurred in a single layer, this would generate a demand for an expected total of 640 interceptors (64 objects times 10 engagements each), but as we saw earlier, by making use of multiple layers we are able to lower the required number of deployed interceptors and, as a consequence, the size of the budget necessary to buy that inventory of interceptors.[16] The question is: how should the ten engagements per surviving warhead be allocated among the layers to yield the lowest cost?

To determine the optimal allocation for a two-layer system, we need to take a step back for a moment. We have discovered that in simple two-layer systems, for certain total demanded numbers of engagements per object (represented here by n and called "transition numbers"), there are two allocations, both of which yield the same least-cost integral solution.[17] For example, as can be seen in Table 2.3, a two-layer system with a demand for nine total engagements per object surviving the defense is at a transition number: two allocations—two engagements per object in the first layer and seven in the second layer (or in shorthand, 2/7) and three in the first layer and six in the second layer (or 3/6)—generate the same least-cost solution of 3.75 interceptors required for each of the attacker's inventory of objects.

Figure 2.5 provides the derivation for transition numbers for the case where $SSPk$ is 1/2 and the costs are equal for both layers.[18]

---

[16]As we will show in Section 5, to hedge against uncertainty in "the luck of the draw," we will want to field more than the expected inventory size of interceptors. So as not to belabor the point, suffice it to say that this applies to all of the optimizations presented herein.

[17]For three-layer systems, there are "transition numbers" which yield three least-cost solutions under certain circumstances. In this report, we have restricted our search for the least-cost firing doctrine to those firing doctrines that result in both an integer number of engagements per object in each layer and an integer number of interceptors deployed in each layer. It is possible, however, to have a nonintegral firing doctrine. For example, 1.5 engagements per presented object can be achieved by putting one engagement on half of the presented objects and two engagements per presented object on the other half.

[18]In general, if x interceptors per attacking object are allocated in the first layer, and y per object in the second layer, the total expected number of interceptors per attacking object is given by $x + q^x y$, where q is $1 - SSPk$. The transitions for a two-layer system occur where

$$n = s + (1 - q^{s+1}) / q^s (1 - q),$$

for which both s and n are integers.

Table 2.3

Required Interceptors for a Two-Layer System

Layer 1 E/PO	Layer 2 E/PO	Total Cost/IO
0	9	9.0
1	8	5.0
2	7	3.75
3	6	3.75
4	5	4.31
5	4	5.13
6	3	6.05
7	2	7.02
8	1	8.0
9	9	9.0

NOTE: $SSPk = 1/2$, one cost unit per assigned interceptor, for all layers. E/PO is engagements per presented object. Total Cost/IO is the expected total cost in interceptors for each of the attacker's inventory of attacking objects.

RANDMR390-2.5

Let:

n = the total demanded number of engagements per object,

$SSPk$ = 1/2 for all layers.

At a transition number, the least-cost solution results with both an allocation of S to the first layer and $n - S$ to the second, and $S + 1$ to the first layer and $n - S - 1$ to the second. Specifically:

$$S + \frac{(n - S)}{2^S} = S + 1 + \frac{(n - S - 1)}{2^{S+1}}$$

$$S[2^{S+1}] + 2[n - S] = 2^{S+1}[S + 1] + n - S - 1$$

$$2n - 2S = 2^{S+1} + n - S - 1$$

$$n = 2^{S+1} + S - 1.$$

Find, for example, the value of n for the transition from $S = 1$ to $S = 2$:

$$n = 2^{S+1} + 1 - 1$$

$$n = 2^2 = 4.$$

Figure 2.5—Derivation of Transition Numbers for Two-Layer Defense

For these numbers, the least-cost solution may be achieved either by an allocation of S engagements in the first layer and $n - S$ engagements in the second layer, or by an allocation of $S+1$ engagements in the first layer and $n - S - 1$ in the second.

Table 2.4 identifies transition points calculated from the formula just presented, for the case of *SSPk* of 1/2 and equal costs per interceptor in all layers.

At these points the number of engagements assigned to the first layer in an optimal allocation is incremented by one, and for every value of *n* between these transition numbers the second-layer engagements per object are incremented by one. The optimal equal-cost integral alternative firing doctrines are presented in Table 2.4's last column, in the form of first-layer allocation/second-layer allocation.[19]

To illustrate, let us return to the problem of how to optimally allocate ten total engagements per surviving object. The optimal solution is to allocate three engagements per object in the first layer and seven in the second layer, that is, 3/7. The number three is gained from the table since the demand is for greater than nine intercepts per surviving object. The number seven is derived by subtracting three from ten. Table 2.5 provides least-cost allocations for from one to twenty total engagements per surviving object for a two-layer defense.

The Optimal Allocation of a Constrained Inventory or Budget

Consider Figure 2.6, which illustrates the second type of optimization problem—finding the allocation that maximizes the probability of no survivors given a constrained inventory or budget. The figure assumes a three-layer defense system with a total available inventory of 192 interceptors, and 64 attacking

Table 2.4

Transition Numbers for a Two-Layer System

First-Layer Allocation (S)	Transition Number n	Optimal Equal-Cost Integral Allocations (first/second layer)
0	$2^{0+1} + 0 - 1 = 1$	0/1 or 1/0
1	$2^{1+1} + 1 - 1 = 4$	1/3 or 2/2
2	$2^{2+1} + 2 - 1 = 9$	2/7 or 3/6
3	$2^{3+1} + 3 - 1 = 18$	3/15 or 4/14
4	$2^{4+1} + 4 - 1 = 35$	4/31 or 5/30
5	$2^{5+1} + 5 - 1 = 68$	5/63 or 6/62
6	$2^{6+1} + 6 - 1 = 133$	6/127 or 7/126
7	$2^{7+1} + 7 - 1 = 262$	7/255 or 8/254

NOTE: *SSPk* = 1/2, one cost unit per assigned interceptor, for all layers.

---

[19]The authors wish to thank RAND colleague David Vaughan for his ingenious and elegant derivation of what we have called "transition numbers," which contributed greatly to our understanding of the phenomenon.

Table 2.5

Optimal Integral Firing Doctrines for Various Total Engagements per Presented Object, Two- and Three-Layer Defenses

Total E/PO	Optimal Integral Firing Doctrines	
	Two-Layer	Three-Layer
1	0/1 or 1/0	0/0/1, 0/1/0, or 1/0/0
2	1/1	0/1/1, 1/0/1, or 1/1/0
3	1/2	1/1/1
4	1/3 or 2/2	1/1/2
5	2/3	1/1/3 or 1/2/2
6	2/4	1/2/3
7	2/5	1/2/4
8	2/6	1/2/5
9	2/7 or 3/6	1/2/6
10	3/7	1/3/6 or 1/2/7
11	3/8	1/3/7
12	3/9	2/3/7
13	3/10	2/3/8
14	3/11	2/3/9
15	3/12	2/3/10
16	3/13	2/3/11
17	3/14	2/3/12
18	3/15 or 4/14	2/3/13
19	4/15	1/2/14
20	4/16	2/4/14 or 2/3/15

NOTE: $SSPk = 1/2$, one cost unit per assigned interceptor, for all layers. Total E/PO is the total engagements per presented object.

objects, thus producing a ratio of inventory engagements to attacking warheads of $192 \div 64 = 3.0$.

Following the figure, the process by which the allocation is done is as follows:

- The first layer is allocated 128 (i.e., 2/3 times 192) of the available interceptors. With two engagements per object in the first layer, an expected $1/2^2 = 1/4$ of 64 or 16 objects penetrate to the second layer.

- In the second layer, we have a ratio of $R = 4.0$ (64 available interceptors for 16 surviving warheads). The algorithm states that we should allocate $(4-1)/4 = 3/4$ of the remaining 64 interceptors (48) to the second layer, for an expected total of three engagements per warhead, and the remaining $64 - 48 = 16$ engagements to subsequent layers.

- In the third layer, with 16 engagements available and $1/32 \cdot 64 = 2$ objects penetrating to the third layer, the ratio of engagements to warheads is $16/2 = 8$.

RAND*MR390-2.6*

Let:

I = the number of deployed interceptors = 192,

W = the number of initial attacking warheads = 64,

R = the ratio of I/W = 3.0,

$SSPk$ = 1/2 for all layers.

Then allocate:

$(R-1)/R$ = 2/3 of 192 or 128 interceptors to the first layer, and

1/3 of 192 = 64 for the remaining layers (two and three).

Repeat the process for the 16 attackers that are expected to survive into

the second layer (with R now equal to 64/16 = 4):

$(R-1)/R$ = 3/4 • 64 = 48 to the second layer, and

$1/R$ = 1/4, therefore 1/4 • 64 = 16 to the third layer.

Figure 2.6—Allocating a Constrained Inventory to a Three-Layer Defense

We now have a total of 13 engagements per surviving object—two in the first layer, three in the second layer, and eight in the third—for a probability of no survivors of $(1 - 0.5^{13})^{64}$ = 99 percent. When the effectiveness of all layers is equal at an $SSPk$ of 1/2, interceptors cost the same for all layers, and there are more interceptors than attacking objects, the allocation of resources according to the algorithm of $(R-1)/R$ provides the optimal allocation (i.e., the highest probability of no survivors) given the available inventory of interceptors.[20]

Some Simple Heuristic Methods Based on Exponential Approximations

We have thus far presented several simple techniques for solving the two optimization problems of interest—finding the least-cost solution for a demanded number of engagements per surviving object, and finding the allocation that maximizes the probability of no survivors given a constrained inventory or budget. We now develop a simple technique for simplifying

---

[20]We have empirically established the optimality condition for the case where $SSPk$ is 1/2; it is our hope that it might be extended beyond this simple form to the more general case.

computations with respect to the "probability of no survivors." The technique involves:

- Using exponential approximations to compute the probability of no survivors of an attacking force.

- Identifying the necessary "margin" of required engagements per object to maintain a demanded level of outcome given an attacking force size.

As will be seen later in this report, these techniques can be quite useful and important in simplifying the analysis of optimum allocation of resources to multilayered defenses.[21]

Approximating the Probability of No Survivors

As described in Figure 2.7, the exponential approximation may be used to approximate the probability of no survivors of an attacking force of missiles.[22] Table 2.6 describes the number of engagements required for greater than 90 percent probability of no survivors when interceptor *SSPk*s are 1/2 and 3/4.

"Margins," the "Rule of Four," and the "Rule of Two"

Consider Figure 2.8, which shows how to use the exponential approximation to estimate the "margin" (the difference between the total number of engagements per object and the exponent of two that estimates the size of the attacking force) necessary to maintain a given probability of no survivors. For *SSPk* of 1/2, to achieve greater than 90 percent probability of no survivors, the number of engagements per surviving object must be four more than the log of the number of attackers to the base two, or a "margin" of four.

If the number of objects is 64 (2^6), for example, then in order to have greater than 90 percent probability of no surviving objects, the number of engagements per surviving object must be ten (6 + 4). This, then, is the "rule of four." If the *SSPk* is 3/4 (rather than 1/2), to have greater than 90 percent probability of no

---

[21]That is, these approximations can simplify "back-of-the-envelope" computations; obviously, given the availability of calculators, microcomputer spreadsheets, and other tools, it is a trivial matter to work out the exact calculations.

[22]We caution the reader that exponential approximations can be poor in some cases, for example, when the number of attacking objects is very small.

RAND*MR390-2.7*

The probability of no survivors is given by:

$$P_0(W) = (1 - (1 - SSPk)^S)^W$$

where S = the total number of engagements per attacking object, and

W = the total number of attacking objects.

This is approximated by $e^{-W(1-SSPk)^S}$, or, letting

$$a = \frac{1}{1 - SSPk}, \text{ equivalently by } e^{-a^{\log_a W - S}}.$$

With $SSPk = 1/2$, 64 attackers, and 6 total engagements per attacker:

$$(1 - (1 - 1/2)^6)^{64} = 0.365.$$

Using the exponential approximation, we find:

$$e^{-(2^6/2^6)} = e^{-1} = 0.368 \sim 0.365.$$

Figure 2.7—Using the Exponential Approximation to Estimate the Probability of No Survivors

Table 2.6

Engagements Required to Achieve >90 Percent Probability of No Surviving Objects

Attacking Objects	Total E/SO	
	$SSPk = 1/2$	$SSPk = 3/4$
8 (2^3)	7	4
16 (2^4)	8	4
32 (2^5)	9	5
64 (2^6)	10	5
128 (2^7)	11	6
256 (2^8)	12	6
512 (2^9)	13	7
1024 (2^{10})	14	7
2048 (2^{11})	15	8
4096 (2^{12})	16	8

NOTE: Total E/SO is the total number of engagements per surviving object.

RAND*MR390-2.8*

$$P_0(W) = (1 - (1 - SSPk)^S)^W.$$

Where $SSPk = 1/2$, the expression reduces to:

$$P_0(W) = [1 - 1/2^S]^W \text{ or, if } 1/2^S \text{ is a small number, we have:}$$

$$P_0(W) \sim e^{-(W/2^S)}.$$

Now rewriting W as $2^{\log_2 W}$,

$$P_0(W) \sim e^{-2^{\log_2 W - S}}.$$

Now find the smallest integral value of the expression $S - \log_2 W$ that yields $>.90$ for $P_0(W)$. That value is 4. That is, if $S - \log_2 W$ is 3, then $P_0(W)$ is .882. But if $S - \log_2 W$ is 4, then $P_0(W)$ is .939, and we find that $S = \log_2 W + 4$.

Figure 2.8—Derivation of the "Rule of Four"

surviving objects the number of engagements per surviving object must be *two* more than the log of the number of objects to the base four—the "rule of two."[23]

Section Summary

The principal insight from the discussion to this point is that it is possible to use a relatively simple parametric formulation for numerically determining—in a simplified analytic setting—the optimal allocation of resources to various layers in a multilayered defense, and to do this taking into account a small number of factors.

The purpose of the next section is to examine more systematically the effects on the optimal firing doctrine, allocation among layers, and cost per object of various factors.

---

[23]In the most general case, we find that $P_0(W) \sim e^{-W(1 - SSPk)^S}$. Obviously, these "rules" are tied to specific *SSPks*, and for other *SSPks*, other "rules" would apply. For example, an *SSPk* of 7/8 would give us the "rule of one." For "back-of-the-envelope" calculations, however, there may be benefits in using *SSPks* that readily translate to "rules" (e.g., 1/2, 3/4, and 7/8).

3. The Principal Cost Drivers of Missile Defense

By now the reader should be familiar with the general logic of the methodology described in this report. The purpose of this section is to gain a better understanding of the factors that drive required inventory size and cost. We will examine the relative importance of four specific factors in sizing a missile defense system:[1]

1. the presence of layering;

2. the size of the attacker's missile inventory;

3. the demanded probability of no survivors; and

4. the effectiveness (*SSPk*) of interceptors in each layer.

Layering

The following "base case"[2] will be used as a point of comparison throughout this section: a three-layer missile defense system defending against 64 attacking objects, with identical *SSPk* of 1/2 for interceptors in each layer, perfect kill assessment assumed, a cost of one for engagements in each layer, and a demand for >90 percent probability of no survivors (i.e., a demand for 10 engagements for each surviving object). Table 3.1 presents various integral firing doctrines in the domain of interest, and their costs.[3]

As shown, among the several optimal (least-cost) solutions is one engagement per object in the first layer, two engagements per object in the second layer, and

---

[1]In Section 4 we will examine four more factors: kill assessment, fractionation, saturation, and "footprint," before assessing the impact of differences in marginal (per interceptor) and buy-in costs.

[2]Designated case A in Table A.1 in the Appendix to this report.

[3]An integral firing doctrine is one that allows only integer values for the number of engagements per object in each layer.

Table 3.1

**Illustrative Firing Doctrines and
Expected Total Inventory Costs**

Firing Doctrine	Expected Total Inventory Cost
0/0/10	640
0/1/9	352
0/2/8	256
0/3/7	248
0/4/6	280
0/5/5	330
1/0/9	352
1/1/8	224
1/2/7	*184*
1/3/6	*184*
1/4/5	202
1/5/4	228
2/0/8	256
2/1/7	200
2/2/6	*184*
2/3/5	186
2/4/4	196

NOTE: 64 attacking objects presented to a three-layer defense system with ten total engagements per surviving attacking object. *SSPk* – 1/2 for each layer. Least-cost optima reported in italics.

seven engagements per object in the third layer—or, in shorthand, 1/2/7—for an expected total inventory requirement of 184 engagements and a cost of 184:[4]

- One engagement against each of the 64 attacking warheads in the first layer, for a total of 64 engagements;

- Two engagements for each of the 32 warheads that on average survive to the second layer, for a total of another 64 engagements; and

- Seven engagements for each of the eight warheads that on average survive the second layer to the third layer, for a total of 56 engagements.

The most important point is that this cost of 184 engagements is significantly (71 percent) lower than the 640 engagements that would have been required if only a single layer were used.[5] Thus, with three layers, we can achieve the demanded

---

[4]As can be seen from the table, there are *three* alternative integral firing doctrines that yield an identical total cost of 184 (reported in italics), but none that produces a lower-cost solution. These three allocations are 1/2/7, 1/3/6, and 2/2/6. These ties suggest that ten total engagements per object is a "transition number" for a three-layer system with an *SSPk* of 1/2 and equal cost of one in all layers.

[5]Case B in Table A.1.

ten engagements per surviving warhead at less than a third of the cost of a one-layer architecture. In short:

- The size of the interceptor inventory necessary to achieve a demanded probability of no survivors is highly sensitive to the existence of multiple look-shoots or layers—*multiple layers can dramatically reduce the size of the inventory of interceptors required to achieve a stated level of outcome*—and all other things being equal, the more layers, the greater the reduction in cost.

Size of the Attacker's Inventory

Figure 3.1 portrays the relationship between the expected total number of interceptors a defender must deploy to attain a probability of no attacking survivors of greater than 90 percent and the size of the attacker's missile inventory. Take, for example, an attacking force of 256 (2^8) missiles. We must now have 12 engagements per surviving object—the rule of four. For the case of a one-layer system this demands an inventory of approximately 3000 interceptors. However, a three-layer system generates a requirement for 760 interceptors (a ratio of about three to one).

Figure 3.2 further emphasizes this point, showing the ratio of the expected interceptors expended to the attack size for optimized layered defenses when the number of attacking objects is varied, and the demanded probability of no survivors is held at greater than 90 percent.[6] As can be seen, both the two- and three-layer systems require far fewer interceptors per attacking object to achieve the demanded outcome than does a one-layer system.

Similarly, from Table 3.2 we can see that increasing the number of attacking objects by a factor of 16 (from 256 to 4096) increases the "ratio" by a factor of only about 1 percent (from 2.97 to 3.09). This again stems from the presence of more than one layer—with one layer, the ratio would have gone from 12 to 16.

The last two figures and the table demonstrate that for multilayered defenses, the "ratio" is quite insensitive to the total number of attacking objects. That is, the expected total number of interceptors to be deployed varies approximately

---

[6]As mentioned earlier, we would actually want to deploy more interceptors to hedge against uncertainty in the "luck of the draw," as we will discuss in Section 5.

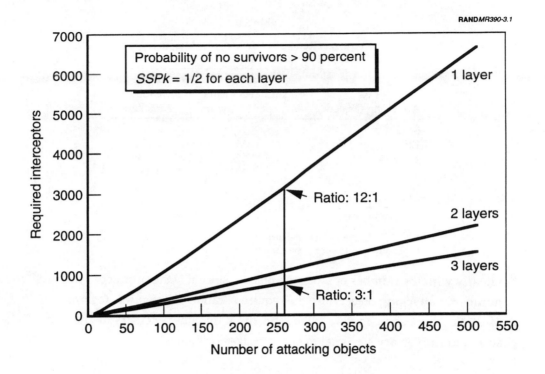

Figure 3.1—Layering Reduces Sensitivity to Attack Size

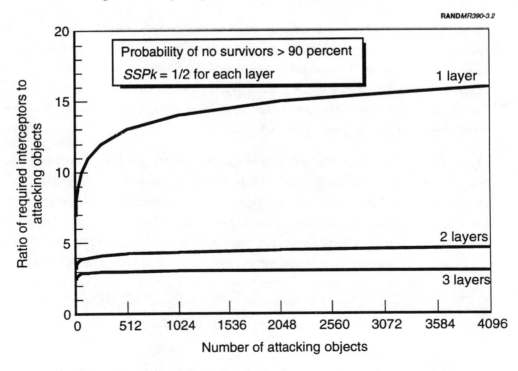

Figure 3.2—Ratio of Required Defender Inventory to Attack Size Given Optimal
Allocation

Table 3.2

Required Ratio of Defenders to Attackers

Number of Attacking Objects	Number of Engagements per Survivor	Required Ratio: Defenders to Attackers
64 (2^6)	10	2.875
128 (2^7)	11	2.938
256 (2^8)	12	2.969
512 (2^9)	13	3.000
1024 (2^{10})	14	3.031
2048 (2^{11})	15	3.063
4096 (2^{12})	16	3.094

NOTE: Three-layer defense system, $SSPk = 1/2$ for each layer. Probability of no survivors >90 percent.

linearly with the number of attacking objects, since it is the product of the number of attacking objects and the required "ratio" of defenders to attackers. Multiple layers serve to reduce the ratio, but it remains necessary to know the size of the adversary's arsenal in order to size our defenses.

Demanded Probability of No Survivors[7]

Similarly, multiple layers have the property of greatly reducing the sensitivity of the cost to a demand for a higher probability of no survivors. As can be seen in Figure 3.3, with a one-layer system, as the total number of engagements per object increases (thus raising the probability of no survivors), the cost rises linearly at a very steep rate. But for the three-layer system, the "cost" flattens out after nine or so engagements per warhead.

Figure 3.4 portrays the relationship between the cost per attacking object and the total number of attacking objects for a three-layer system and two different single-shot kill probabilities. As just discussed, we see that for the three-layer system, cost is relatively insensitive to the probability of no survivors, there being little difference in cost between probabilities of 94 percent and 1.8 percent. We find this both counterintuitive and important—it says that with a multilayered defense, tightening the demand for no survivors can be achieved at a relatively small increase in expected total system cost. We will now describe in a bit more detail how the demand for a higher probability of no survivors drives (1) the

---

[7]In addition to the probability of no survivors, some readers may also wish to keep track of the expected number of objects leaking through the missile defense system. The relationship between p(no leakers) and the number of leakers is a very simple mathematical identity: $-p = e^{-x}$, where p is the probability of no survivors and x is the expected number of leakers. Taking the case of 64 attackers, $SSPk$ of 1/2, and .939 probability of no leakers, since $p = .939$, we find that $x = .0625$, since $.939 = e^{-.0625}$.

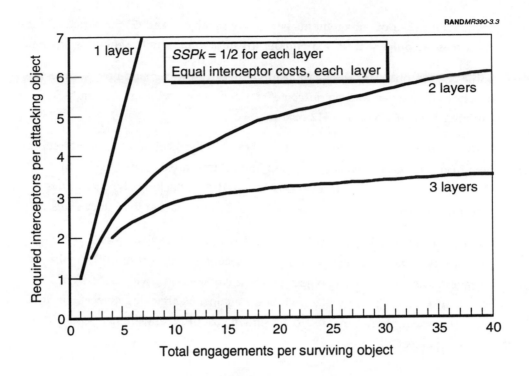

Figure 3.3—Layering Reduces Cost per Attacking Warhead

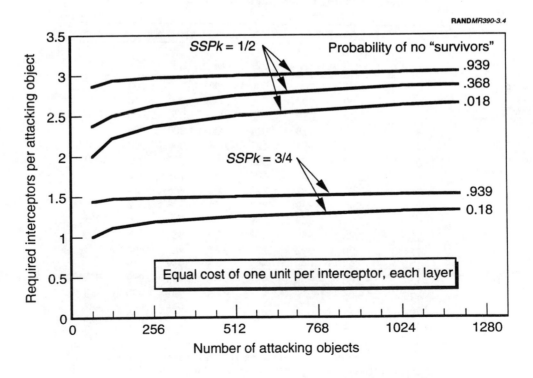

Figure 3.4—Cost per Attacking Object Is Sensitive to Probability of Kill

required number of engagements per surviving object; and (2) the expected total resources the defense must expend per inventory object in the enemy's arsenal.

Table 3.3 demonstrates the relationship between "the demand on resources" as a function of "the demand on outcome"; it does so for various sizes of attack (ranging from 16 objects to 512 objects).

To orient the reader, the column titled "I/SO" is the total number of interceptors per surviving object that is demanded; the column titled "Expected Total Cost/IO" is the expected resources demanded per attacking object; and the columns headed 16, 32, and so on, reflect different attacker inventory sizes.

Take, for example, the case of 64 attacking objects. To register a positive probability of zero leakage (at least in the second significant figure) requires four engagements per surviving object, i.e., four engagements with an *SSPk* of 1/2 results in a .02 probability of zero leakage against 64 attacking objects. In turn, the four engagements require a deployment cost of 2.0 engagements per attacking object.

Table 3.3

Probability of No Survivors as a Function of "Engagements per Surviving Object" and "the Number of Attackers"

I/SO	Expected Total Cost/IO	Number of Attackers					
		16	32	64	128	256	512
0	0.00	.000	.000	.000	.000	.000	.000
1	1.00	.000	.000	.000	.000	.000	.000
2	1.40	.010	.000	.000	.000	.000	.000
3	1.70	.118	.014	.000	.000	.000	.000
4	2.00	.356	.127	.016	.000	.000	.000
5	2.20	.602	.362	.131	.017	.000	.000
6	2.40	.777	.604	.365	.133	.017	.000
7	2.50	.882	.778	.605	.366	.134	.018
8	2.60	.939	.882	.778	.606	.367	.135
9	2.70	.969	.939	.882	.779	.606	.368
10	2.85	.985	.969	.939	.882	.778	.606
11	2.90	.992	.985	.969	.939	.883	.778
12	2.95	.996	.992	.985	.969	.939	.883
13	3.00		.996	.992	.985	.969	.939
14	3.05			.996	.992	.985	.969
15	3.10				.996	.992	.985
16	3.15					.996	.992
17	3.20						.996

NOTE: *SSPk* = 1/2. I/SO is interceptors per surviving object.
Expected Total Cost/IO is the total cost per attacker's inventory object.

At the same time, we observe from the table, still for the case of 64 attacking objects, that a demand for a probability of no survivors of 94 percent requires 10 engagements per surviving object—an increase by a factor of 2.5 in terms of total engagements (10 divided by 4). However, the expected demand on deployed resources is increased by only a factor of 1.425 (2.85 divided by 2).

Now examine the relative increase in expected deployment costs for the case of 512 objects. The demand of .02 probability of success places an expected demand for deployed resources of 2.5 engagements per inventory object. A demand of .94 probability of success places a demand on deployed resources of 3.00 engagements per inventory object. The increase here is a factor of 1.2. That is, for a 20 percent increase in deployed resources, the probability of success is raised from a dismal .02 to a highly respectable .94.

The table shows that for these numbers of attacking objects, a shift upward in probability of success from .02 to .94 results from adding six engagements per surviving object. (From 4 to 10 for 64 attacking objects and from 7 to 13 for 512 attacking objects.) But this shift in engagements per surviving object does not cause a commensurate increase in deployment costs (cost per inventory object). The table also shows that the dynamic range for the "cost per object" is not great, from around 2.0 for small numbers of attackers and low demands on outcome to 3.0 for large numbers of attackers and robust demands on outcome.

For the case of "optimized" multilayered defenses, since the cost for a high probability of zero leakage is not much more than that for a low probability (e.g., for increases in deployment costs of well under 50 percent more, we can afford a high probability of no survivors), it seems sensible to demand a high probability of zero leakers. Accordingly, in the analyses in this report, we will demand at least 90 percent probability of zero leakers.

Effectiveness of Interceptors in Each Layer

It is clear from Figure 3.4 that higher interceptor effectiveness (*SSPk*) *does* greatly reduce the cost per attacking object. There is a large difference in cost corresponding to the cases of *SSPk* = 1/2 and *SSPk* = 3/4. How kill probability affects the optimal allocation, however, is somewhat complex.

Consider our base case of 64 attacking warheads against a three-layer system, where *SSPk* = 1/2 and per-shot cost is one in all layers, with a demand for >90 percent probability of no survivors. The optimal allocation in this case is the firing doctrine of 1/2/7, for an average allocation of 64 engagements in the first layer, 64 in the second, and 56 in the third, or an expected total of 184 engagements. The implications of higher and lower *SSPk* in the first layer are as follows:

- *Case C in Table A.1.* If the *SSPk* in the first layer is, for example, 3/4—higher than the *SSPk* of 1/2 in other layers—the optimal allocation is 1/2/6: there is no change in the number of engagements per object in the first layer, but a reduction in the total number of engagements per object in later layers, with all of the reduction (from seven to six) taking place in the last layer. The new allocation is 64 engagements in the first layer, 32 in the second, and 24 in the third, for an expected total of 120 engagements, a reduction of 64 interceptors from the base case.[8]

- *Case D in Table A.1.* However, when the effectiveness of the first layer is 1/4, the optimal allocation still places one engagement per object in the first layer, two in the second, and seven in the third, or 1/2/7. This translates to 64 engagements in the first layer, 96 engagements in the second layer, and 84 in the third, for an expected total of 244 engagements, 60 more than the base case.

Based upon this simple parametric analysis, it should be clear that the effectiveness of interceptors is a significant factor in overall inventory requirements and costs.

Section Summary

In this section we have examined a great many cases, summarized in Table A.1 in the Appendix. We began by examining the impact of four factors on required inventory size and, by implication, overall missile defense costs:

1. the number of layers of the missile defense system;

2. the size of the attacker's inventory;

3. the demanded probability of no survivors; and

4. the effectiveness of the interceptors in each layer (*SSPk*).

Through these analyses, we determined that an optimized layered defense is an effective means of reducing the costs of a missile defense system. Such defenses reduce the required ratio of deployed interceptors to attackers, thereby reducing

---

[8]The lower number of interceptors required in the successive layers arises from the fact that each interceptor in the first layer has twice the effectiveness; rather than 32 objects surviving the first layer, only 16 now do, lowering the required number of engagements to achieve the demanded probability of no survivors.

the required inventory of interceptors. Multiple layers can contribute greatly to reducing the growth rate of the required interceptor inventory, thus yielding a high probability of zero leakers without having to incur much additional cost. Finally, *SSPk* of interceptors remains a significant driver of the total cost per inventory object. Throughout, we have shown that a simplified analytic framework may be used to examine the impact of these various parameters.

In the next section we will turn our focus to some operational parameters that also have an impact on the overall cost of a missile defense system.

4. Operational Cost Drivers

In addition to the four factors we identified in the last section, four additional considerations, of an operational nature, drive the optimal allocation of resources to layered defenses:

5. the quality of kill assessment;

6. fractionation;

7. saturation and exhaustion; and

8. multiple terminal sites to provide a "footprint."

Quality of Kill Assessment

To understand the problem of kill assessment, we need to provide two additional definitions before we may proceed:

- The "probability of surviving" ($SSPs$) is defined as $1 - SSPk$.

- The "probability of leaking" ($SSPl$) is defined as the probability that an object will be targeted for an engagement in the next "look-shoot," given an engagement by a single interceptor in the prior "look-shoot."[1]

If "kill assessment" is perfect, then the "probability of leaking" is exactly the same as "the probability of surviving" ($1 - SSPk$). If 1/2 of the objects in an attack are killed in a particular "look-shoot," then with perfect kill assessment, the 1/2 of the objects not killed are seen and engaged by the next "look-shoot." With perfect kill assessment, if 3/4 are killed, 1/4 leak to the next layer.

On the other hand, if "kill assessment" is not perfect, then the next "look-shoot" will see and engage more objects than indicated by the probability of surviving. For example, a particular "shoot" might indeed kill 1/2 of the attacking objects, but because of less-than-perfect "kill assessment," the next "look-shoot" might see and engage 3/4 of the objects that were in the previous layer (all of those not killed and 1/2 of those that were killed). That is, of the objects attacked in the next "look-shoot," 1/3 of them have already been killed but are nevertheless

---

[1] Also referred to as the "leakage rate." By definition, $SSPk \geq 1 - SSPl$.

engaged. Table 4.1 shows how imperfect kill assessment can affect the cost in interceptors per attacking object.[2]

There is, ultimately, a reliable method for determining whether an object has been killed. If the object hits (or falls) near the target and the warhead detonates, the object was not killed. If not, the object is deemed as killed. Eventually, things are sorted out on the ground. Thus, in computing the probability of no operational weapons impacting at or near the targets, the "probability of kill" in each layer is the relevant measure of effectiveness. For example, if the "probability of kill" is 1/2 and there are 512 (2^9) attacking objects, then using the "rule of four," we see that we need 13 engagements per surviving object in order to have more than 90 percent probability of no weapons "operating" (exploding) on friendly soil. On the other hand, the "probability of leaking" ($SSPl$), as defined here, is the appropriate measure to use in determining *how many interceptors must be deployed* by the defender and the proper allocation of those interceptors among layers. The table captures the logic just described.

The above construction takes into account three cases and neglects one. It takes into account:

1. the objects not destroyed in one layer and engaged by the next;
2. the objects destroyed in one layer and not engaged by the next; and
3. the objects destroyed in one layer but still engaged by the next.

Table 4.1

Increase in Expected Total Cost per Attacking Object for Two-Layer System in the Absence of Perfect Kill Assessment

Engagements per Surviving Object	Total Cost/IO	
	$SSPl = 1/2$	$SSPl = 3/4$
10	3.875	5.90
11	4.000	6.21
12	4.125	6.53
13	4.250	6.85

NOTE: $SSPk = 1/2$, one cost unit per assigned interceptor, for all layers. Optimal allocations assumed. The case of $SSPl = 1/2$ means there is perfect kill assessment since then $SSPl = 1 - SSPk$. Total Cost/IO is the expected total cost in interceptors for each of the attacker's inventory of attacking objects.

[2]Imperfect kill assessment will also change the optimal allocation: in the case of ten shots per surviving object, the allocation with perfect kill assessment (where $SSPl$ and $SSPk$ are identical at 1/2) is 3/7, but when $SSPl$ is 3/4 and $SSPk$ is 1/2, the optimal allocation is 4/6.

The construction does not take into account the case where an object is not killed in one layer and is not evaluated for engagement in the next layer.

The rules of engagement will be such as to mandate an engagement unless there is clear evidence that the object has already been killed; when in doubt, an engagement should be attempted. Because of this imperative, the number of objects in the set of those not destroyed in one layer and not engaged in the next should be quite small. If this fraction is at all significant, however, the "probability of no survivors" will be quite small.

Recall that the probability of leaking ($SSPl$) identifies the percent of objects that the next layer sees, independent of whether they have been killed. Up to this point, we have generally assumed that probability of survival ($1 - SSPk$) and probability of leaking ($SSPl$) were identical, i.e., that the $SSPk$ represented the probability that a single engaged warhead would not "leak" to the next layer. We will now relax this assumption and introduce the notion that the survival rate and leakage rate may differ, sometimes significantly.

The survival and leakage rates may differ when an object "killed" in one layer is nevertheless engaged by the next layer, i.e., the kill assessment system is unable to distinguish perfectly between objects that have been killed and those that haven't. Let us briefly consider the physical problem to understand the circumstances under which the survival and leakage rates might differ.

- During a missile's prelaunch period, whether it is in a factory, in garrison, en route to a launching site, or mounted on a transporter-erector-launcher (TEL), a kill on the ground will keep the missile from being seen by sensors and targeting systems in the boost-phase layer because it will be rendered unlaunchable.[3]

- Similarly, during boost phase, before threat missile burnout and entry into ballistic trajectory, a kill will result in a disrupted trajectory, causing the missile to fall back to earth far short of its intended target, unseen (or else clearly assessed) by the next layer of midcourse look-shoots.

- After burnout, the missile is on a ballistic trajectory. A kill here may or may not result in the missile's being engaged by the next layer. That is, at this point missiles whose warheads have been disabled or destroyed may be very hard to distinguish from those that have not been killed; the kinematics of "killed" and "not-killed" missiles may appear similar.

---

[3]For a discussion of some of the virtues of boost-phase defenses, see Stephen Weiner, "Systems and Technology," in Ashton B. Carter and David N. Schwartz (eds.), *Ballistic Missile Defense*, Washington, D.C.: The Brookings Institution, 1984, pp. 49–97 and especially pp. 91–97.

- By late midcourse and terminal phases, the continued ballistic trajectories of "killed" missiles (or objects) may make it impossible to distinguish between killed objects and those objects that have not been killed; every object penetrating to the last layer, killed or not, represents a threat and is probably engaged.

The way we treat this problem is to use the parameters, $SSPk$ and $SSPl$, in the following way:

- $SSPk$ will still be used to determine the *required number of engagements per attacking warhead* to achieve the demanded probability of no survivors.[4]

- $SSPl$ will be used to determine the *size of the inventory required* to achieve the necessary number of engagements.[5] That is, lack of kill assessment places a demand for more deployed interceptors, but it does not affect our computation of the probability of no survivors.

Case E in Table A.1. Let us assume that in the second layer, although the $SSPk$ remains 1/2 and costs remain the same, there is a 75 percent leakage rate ($SSPl = 3/4$) due to the fact that it is very difficult to distinguish between vehicles killed in the second layer and those not killed. The optimal solution for this excursion puts two engagements per object in the first layer, two in the second, and six in the third layer (a firing doctrine of 2/2/6), for a total of 128 interceptors in the first layer, 32 in the second, and 54 interceptors in the third.[6] The allocation reduces the number of objects that leak into the second layer, where the effectiveness is weaker. Furthermore, the poor effectiveness of assessing "kills" after the middle layer drives the minimum required engagements up from 184 to 214, a cost increase of 16 percent, and allocates a great deal more interceptors to the first layer, where the leakage rate equals $(1 - SSPk)$.

Figure 4.1 portrays the number of interceptors a defender must deploy to achieve >90 percent probability of no survivors as a function of the number of attacking objects. There are two pairs of lines: the topmost pair represents the two-layer missile defense system, and the bottom pair represents a three-layer system. For each pair, the solid line represents the case of perfect kill assessment, where $SSPk$ and $SSPl$ have identical values of 1/2 in all layers, and the dashed line reflects the cases when $SSPk$ is 1/2 and the leakage rate ($SSPl$) in the next-to-last layer is

---

[4]The computation becomes more complex if the $SSPk$s are different in each layer because of the various combinations that might yield an equivalent probability of no leakers.

[5]That is, $SSPl$ is substituted for $1 - SSPk$ in the allocation optimization process.

[6]A firing doctrine of 2/3/5 yields a lower cost per attacking object (3.277), but it results in 33.75 interceptors allocated to the last layer—an impossibility.

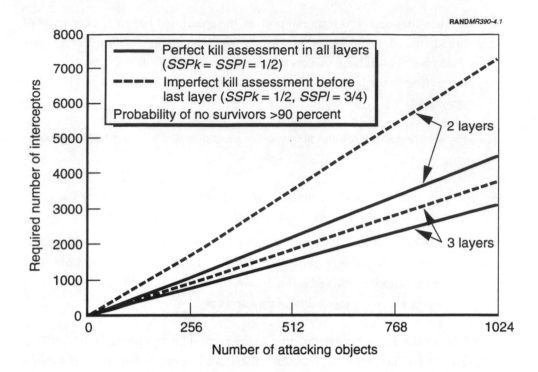

Figure 4.1—The Effect of Imperfect Kill Assessment

higher—at 3/4. As is clear from the figure, imperfect kill assessment, resulting in a higher leakage rate, can increase the size of the inventory of interceptors required to achieve a demanded probability of no survivors, because subsequent layers fire at more objects, some of which have already been killed. The effect is much more pronounced in a two-layer system than in a three-layer system.[7]

Fractionation

Fractionation—the dispensing of submunitions or multiple warheads—greatly complicates the planning of missile defenses and can greatly increase system costs. That is, fractionation multiplies the number of attacking objects that the next layers must engage and thus increases the effective size of an adversary's attack.

We will use the term "prefractionation" to connote operations during the time before submunitions separate from their missile. This is meant to include consideration of a whole range of prelaunch operations (including special

---

[7]Clearly, additional sensitivity analyses on kill assessment and discrimination would be useful, but they are well beyond the scope of this report.

operations and counterforce), as well as boost and postboost intercepts taking place before fractionation.

Case F in Table A.1. Take the following case: a demand for at least 90 percent probability of total threat negation, three layers, with *SSPk* of 1/2, a cost of one in each layer, and fractionation by a factor of 16 after the first layer. That is, a missile not killed in the first layer will fractionate into 16 objects (submunitions and/or decoys) that must be faced by the next layer.[8] For this case, the optimum firing doctrine is 6/2/6, at a cost of 440 engagements: 384 engagements in the first layer, 32 in the second layer, and 24 in the last layer, for a total cost of 6.875 per attacking object—fractionation has required additional resources, most of which are allocated to the prefractionation layer. As expected, because of fractionation, the allocation emphasizes the first layer because of the leverage provided by early intercept—and the cost penalty in fielding systems to defend against the expanded number of attacking objects after fractionation.

Figure 4.2 plots the optimal allocation of engagements among three layers as a function of the level of fractionation. The key insight for the figure is that it is extremely efficient to allocate resources to kills before fractionation—as described by the figure, as fractionation increases, allocating interceptors to the layer before fractionation keeps an even larger number of warheads or submunitions from surviving and leaking into the next layer. As the fractionation rate increases the number of engagements in the last two layers remains constant, and the first layer (before fractionation) is allocated additional engagements.

Further, there are numerous additional operational reasons that argue for attacking missiles before fractionation. Because of the smaller size and greater number of submunitions, once fractionation has taken place it may be virtually impossible to distinguish between submunitions that have been rendered ineffective and those that haven't. The use of decoys may further complicate postfractionation defenses, making prefractionation intercepts more attractive.[9]

---

[8]With 64 initial attackers and a fractionation factor of 16, this would yield 1024 fractionated objects if none of the missiles were destroyed before fractionation. The reader will recall that by the "rule of four," 1024 attackers against interceptors having an *SSPk* of 1/2 generates a demand for 14 engagements per object (1024 is 2^{10}, and ten plus four is 14) for >90 percent probability of total threat negation.

[9]Jasper Welch has noted that we may also prefer prefractionation intercept because there may be difficulties associated with multiple engagements of objects once they are in ballistic trajectory. While it would clearly appear to be a useful area for additional analysis, it is well beyond the scope of this report to address the issue in detail.

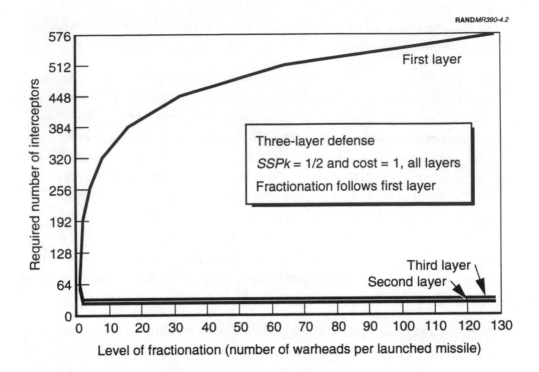

RAND*MR390-4.2*

Figure 4.2—The Effect of Fractionation on the Optimal Allocation

Saturation and Exhaustion

A third operational issue is that of saturation, where an attacking missile force may be of sufficient size to overwhelm missile defenses. We now address this problem, especially with regard to boost/prefractionation systems.

One construct is the following terms: the role of boost and postboost defenses is to reduce, *over the campaign*, the expected total number of objects seen and engaged by the midcourse and terminal defenses. It is in the last "look-shoot" layers that the demanded number of engagements for each surviving object is enforced.[10] In this construct, the phrase "over the campaign" takes on special importance. If the boost and postboost systems can reduce the number of objects that would otherwise be seen and engaged by subsequent layers by one-half, for example, then the defender can reduce the number of interceptors deployed in subsequent layers by slightly more than one-half. We will now show why this is so.

---

[10]Recall that the demanded number of engagements per surviving object is determined by the requirement to achieve a stated probability that no operating weapons will penetrate all defense layers.

Consider the case of 64 attackers, a three-layer defense system where the last two layers have an *SSPk* of 1/2, a cost of one for each interceptor, and perfect kill assessment. If there are no engagements in the first layer, then these two layers see 64 attackers, and the optimal firing doctrine is 3/7 for the last two layers (see Table 2.4). The expected total required inventory of interceptors is 192 in the second layer and 56 in the last layer, for a total of 248.

Suppose the first layer (representing boost and prefractionation defense) is able to reduce, over the campaign, the number of attackers reaching layer two from 64 to 32. Then only nine engagements per surviving object are required, with the optimal firing doctrine being 2/7, and an expected total cost of 120 ($32 \cdot 2 + 8 \cdot 7$), plus the costs for prefractionation defenses.[11]

In terms of sizing the required inventory, the most important issue is whether, over the course of the campaign, the boost and prefractionation defenses can live up to their "contract" to kill a stated percentage of the total attacking objects— even though they may occasionally be out of position or temporarily be saturated in a particular attack and thus unable to engage all attacking missiles.

With respect to boost/prefractionation defenses, the defender's concern is not about temporary saturation or being out of position in a particular attack.[12] Rather, his worry is in another direction: if the defender is counting on the boost and prefractionation defenses to subtract out half the objects over the campaign, and they actually subtract out only a third, then there is a higher probability that midcourse and terminal defenses will run out of interceptors before the campaign is over.

On the other hand, the defender must worry about saturation in the last layer and plan the architecture accordingly. Previous layers prevent exhaustion in the last layer and should help alleviate saturation in that layer, i.e., in the presence of previous layers, the attacker does not have complete control of the rate of presentation of objects to the last layer.

In summary, the problem of saturation is most relevant in the last "look-shoot." Prior "look-shoots" have the task of reducing the total number of objects according to their "contract" so that defenses in the next layers do not run out of interceptors during the campaign.

---

[11]We will later devote a section to an illustrative mission area analysis that includes tradeoffs between boost/prefractionation and postfractionation defenses.

[12]Although in the case of nuclear weapons, this would obviously be an important concern.

40

Multiple Sites to Provide a "Footprint"

Case G in Table A.1. Now consider the case where eight terminal defense sites are required in the last layer to adequately defend a designated "footprint," and for simplifying purposes, there is no overlap in defense coverage among the sites. The demanded probability of no survivors remains at greater than 90 percent, and the *SSPk* and costs of interceptors are identical in each layer. Table 4.2 shows a worksheet for the case.

We can see that for the three-layer system, the optimal allocation is 2/5/3, which results in 128 interceptors in the first layer, 80 in the second layer, and 12 in the last layer, and the expected total interceptors deployed increase from the base case of 184 to 220. The existence of separate sites is somewhat similar to fractionation: allocations prior to the terminal layer become more attractive.

Section Summary

Although the analysis in this section has led to the inclusion of a number of new parameters, we have shown that the methodology can readily incorporate them, and issues of an operational nature can be assessed with minimal changes to the basic framework. In this section we have showed how the methodology could be used to examine the quality of kill assessment, fractionation, saturation and

Table 4.2

Worksheet for Determining the Least-Cost Defense Allocation, Eight Terminal Defense Sites

Layer									Total	Expected Total
1st			2nd			3rd				
f	I/O	c	f	I/O	c	f	I/O	c	I/O	Cost/Object
			1	0	1·0=0	1	10	1·10·8	10	80
			1	1	1	1/2	9	36	10	37
			1	2	2	1/4	8	16	10	18
			1	3	3	1/8	7	7	10	10
			1	4	4	1/16	6	3	10	7
			1	**5**	**5**	**1/32**	**5**	**1.25**	10	**6.25**
			1	6	6	1/64	4	.5	10	6.5
1	0	0	1	5	5	1/32	5	1.25	10	6.25
1	1	1	1/2	5	5/2	1/64	4	.5	10	4
1	**2**	**2**	**1/4**	**5**	**5/4**	**1/128**	**3**	**.19**	**10**	**3.44**
1	3	3	1/8	5	5/8	1/256	2	.07	10	3.69

NOTE: 64 attacking objects. *SSPk* = 1/2, cost of one per assigned interceptor, for all layers. Eight sites with four interceptors at each site in terminal layer. Preferred allocations in bold.

exhaustion, and multiple sites—and this has led to additional insights on resource allocation:

- The quality of kill assessment determines the number of additional interceptors that must be bought to ensure that the demanded number of engagements can be achieved.
- Fractionation increases our preference for allocating interceptors to layers before fractionation, and away from postfractionation defenses.

In the next section, we will explain how the optimal allocation of resources is affected by differences in layer interceptor costs and buy-in costs, and then we will present an excursion in which a number of parameters are simultaneously varied from their base case value.

5. Interceptor and Buy-In Costs

In addition to the eight factors we have thus far examined, there are two cost-related considerations that also drive the optimal allocation of resources to layered defenses:

9. the case where there are differences in the per-interceptor costs from layer to layer; and

10. the case where there are buy-in costs that must be assumed before any interceptors can be deployed.

Since each of the excursions we have described in the past sections has examined the impact of a single factor somewhat in isolation of the remaining ones, this section concludes with the analysis of a case that involves simultaneously changing several assumptions from the base case values.

Different Interceptor Costs in Each Layer

Consider two additional excursions: in the first, the cost per engagement in the first layer is twice that in the other two layers; in the second, the cost per interceptor in the first layer is half the cost in the other layers. Remember that the base case yielded an optimal allocation of 1/2/7 and 184 total interceptors for achieving >90 percent probability of no survivors.

- *Case H in Table A.1.* The case where the cost in the first layer is twice that in the other layers has an allocation identical to the case where the effectiveness of the first layer was half that of the other layers, a firing doctrine of 0/3/7, for an expected total inventory of 248 interceptors—as compared to the base case of 184 interceptors.

- *Case I in Table A.1.* When the cost in the first layer is half that of the other layers, the firing doctrine is 2/2/6 for an expected inventory size of 184 interceptors. The total expected number of interceptors required is the same as the base case—184. However, since the 128 interceptors in the first layer come at half the normal price, the expected resources to be expended is reduced from the base case—from 2.875 units of cost per enemy inventory missile to 1.875.

Not surprisingly, the effects are somewhat similar to the cases where the effectiveness of the first layer was varied (but the unit cost was the same in each layer)—resources are allocated away from the more expensive layer.

Buy-In Costs

We generally consider costs to be somewhat "lumpy" and to reflect not just the cost of the interceptors, but the costs of an "engagement," which also includes some of the associated infrastructure and support: sensors, engagement control systems, launchers, operations and support, etc. One can dynamically determine the costs of units over various numbers of attacking warheads[1] in one of two ways:

- by rolling all investment and other fixed costs into cost per interceptor, and thereby amortizing the fixed costs over the deployed interceptors; or
- by separating out fixed costs from marginal costs.[2]

As will be seen, the way buy-in costs are treated has significant implications for the optimal allocation of resources.

Buy-In Costs in One Layer

Consider another excursion to the base case, where there are fixed buy-in costs that must be assumed before the first interceptor can be fielded. Assume 64 attacking objects against a three-layer system, but assume that the first layer has a buy-in cost of 512 cost units and there is no buy-in cost for the other two layers.[3] Again, the objective is to ensure at least a 90 percent probability of zero leakage.

If we were to use the base case allocation of 1/2/7, the inventory cost for the three-layer system would climb from 184 to 696, 512 of which would be accounted for by the buy-in cost in the first layer. Because of this buy-in cost, however, the re-optimized allocation for 64 attackers is weighted away from the first layer, and it results in an allocation of 0/3/7 and no interceptors to the first

---

[1]One may also use a hybrid approach in which some costs (e.g., operations and support, individual batteries' equipment sets) are rolled into the unit cost, and some (e.g., research and development, portions of theater sensor systems) are considered as fixed costs and amortized over the total inventory of units. This approach is not developed here.

[2]Since our measure of merit is cost per attacking object.

[3]This could reflect the fact that production of the systems in the other layers is already at production cost, and that fixed costs have already been covered.

layer, 192 to the second layer, and 56 to the third layer, at an expected total cost of 248.

The aversion to incurring the buy-in cost for the first layer diminishes as the attack size increases, however, because the buy-in costs are amortized over the larger number of attacking warheads. Figure 5.1 portrays the optimal allocation of interceptors given a buy-in cost of 512 in the first layer, as just described, but at different numbers of attacking missiles. As can be seen from the figure, for fewer than 512 attacking missiles, there are insufficient attackers to warrant paying the buy-in cost in the first layer. At 512 attacking objects, however, we are indifferent between interceptors bought in the first or second layer, and with more than 512 attackers, the first layer is allocated most of the new interceptors.[4]

Identical Buy-In Costs in All Layers

The case where there are identical buy-in and marginal costs in each layer is somewhat more complicated: a buy-in cost in all layers means that each layer

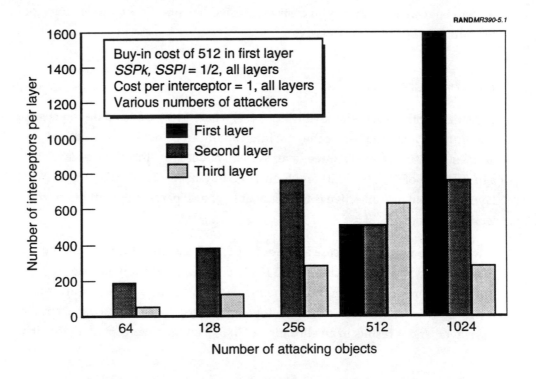

Figure 5.1—Buy-In Costs in One Layer

---

[4]With lower buy-in costs the same threshold phenomenon would be observed, although the threshold for affordably buying into new layers would obviously be lower.

45

faces a threshold, the net effect of which is that it makes multiple layers of look-shoots more costly. That is, buy-in costs in all layers may negate some of the cost advantages of multiple layers by making the cost for an additional layer prohibitively expensive.

Consider another excursion to the base case, this time where there are buy-in costs of 512 for each of the three layers. The base case allocation of 1/2/7 would have resulted in an inventory cost of 1720 units, because we would first have to pay the buy-in costs for each of the layers (for an expected total of 1536) before buying the 184 engagements.

As shown in Figure 5.2, however, when the allocation is reoptimized for the buy-in costs in all layers, the optimal allocation is the firing doctrine of 0/0/10, for a total of no engagements in the first and second layers and 640 engagements in the third, at a total expected inventory cost of 1152. Thus, at 64 attackers, the buy-in costs for three separate layers might be prohibitively expensive, mitigating against multiple layers; it is most efficient to assume the buy-in cost for only a single layer. Nevertheless, and as might be expected from the case of buy-in costs for a single layer, at successively higher numbers of attackers, it becomes cost-effective to absorb the buy-in costs and field interceptors in

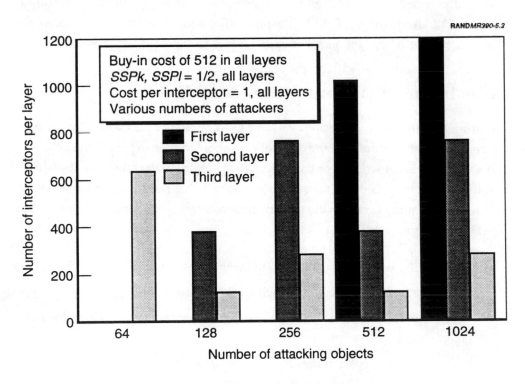

Figure 5.2—Buy-In Costs in All Layers

additional layers. In fact, if the number of attacking objects were 128, fielding a second layer would reduce the expected total cost. With just one layer the cost is 1408 (128 · 11) plus the 512 buy-in for the first layer. With two layers, the firing doctrine is 3/8 and the expected cost is 512 plus 512, or 1024.

Buy-In in the Presence of Fractionation

Emphasizing prefractionation defenses remains attractive even when there may be considerable buy-in costs in fielding that layer. Take the case of 64 missiles with a fractionation into 16 submunitions after the first layer. For the case of a defense that includes a prefractionation layer, the cost of the optimally allocated defense is 440 (see Case F in Table A.1). On the other hand, if there were no prefractionation layer, the cost of the deployed defense would be much greater, since the number of attacking objects is 1024 (64 · 16). Fourteen engagements per surviving object are required to achieve >90 percent probability of no survivors. The optimal firing doctrine is 3/11 (see Table 2.4). The allocation of engagements is 3072 to the penultimate layer and 1408 to the last layer, for a total expected number of engagements of 4480.

The difference between 4480 and 440 interceptors is much greater than the buy-in cost of 512. Accordingly, fielding the prefractionation layer, even in the presence of a large buy-in cost, represents a large savings in expected total resources.

Illustration of a More Complicated Case

Throughout the last two sections we have used rather simple cases to better show how each parameter affects the optimal allocation and the expected total costs. We will now use a worksheet-based approach similar to the one used elsewhere in this report to consider a more complicated case that reflects simultaneously differences among layers in the effectiveness of interceptors, the leakage rate, and per- interceptor costs (this is Case J in Table A.1):

- 64 attacking warheads against a two-layer system.

- $SSPk = 1/2$ in the first layer and $SSPk = 3/4$ in the second layer.

- $SSPl = 3/4$ from the first layer to the second layer (not applicable in the last layer).

- Per-engagement costs in the second layer are twice those of the first layer, i.e., the higher effectiveness of interceptors in the last layer comes at twice the price.

- Assume finally that we demand a greater than 90 percent probability of no survivors and want to find the least-cost solution.

First, if the *SSPk* were 1/2 in both layers, 64 attacking objects would require ten engagements per surviving object to achieve a demanded outcome of greater than 90 percent, and the optimal allocation in a two-layered system would be 3/7—three engagements per object in the first layer, and seven per object in the second. Given a different effectiveness of interceptors in each layer, we first need to determine how many engagements per object are required to achieve the demanded probability of no survivors.

Figure 5.3 provides a formula for computing the probability of no survivors when the effectiveness varies from layer to layer. As can be seen, the probability of no survivors is determined by layer effectiveness and the number of shots fired in each layer. However, we know from the "rule of four" that with engagements having an effectiveness of 1/2, we need a total of $\log_2 64 + 4 = 10$ engagements per surviving object to achieve a >90 probability of no survivors, and from the "rule of two" that with engagements having an effectiveness of 3/4, we need half as many ($5 = \log_4 64 + 2$) engagements per surviving object to achieve the same level of outcome.

We therefore start the first row of the worksheet in Table 5.1 by placing ten engagements per surviving attack object in the first layer and none in the second, and placing in the last row no engagements per object in the first layer and five in the second layer.[5] The costs per object for each allocation are in the column titled "*c*" and are computed as that layer's product of the fraction of the initial attack seen, the number of engagements per object, and the cost per engagement. The expected total cost per object is merely the sum of the costs in the two layers.

In allocating different combinations of engagements per object between the first and second layer, we know (or can infer) from the "rule of four" and "rule of two" that when the effectiveness of the second layer is twice that of the first, two engagements in the first layer are equivalent to one engagement in the second. We can therefore fill in the various allocations at a 2:1 tradeoff between the first and second layer (e.g., 10/0, 8/1, 6/2), all of which achieve the demanded probability of no survivors.[6]

---

[5]As introduced in Table 2.1, *f* denotes the fraction of the initial attack "seen" by the indicated layer, and E/O denotes engagements per attacking object in that layer.

[6]The reader may wish to confirm that the demanded probability of no survivors is being achieved by computing the probability with the formula presented in Figure 5.3.

RAND*MR390-5.3*

For n layers of look-shoots, the probability of no survivors is given by:

$$P_0(W) = [1 - ((1 - SSPk_1)^{S_1} \cdot (1 - SSPk_2)^{S_2} \cdot \ldots \cdot (1 - SSPk_n)^{S_n})]^W$$

where:

$SSPk_l$ = single-shot kill probability in layer l,

S_l = number of interceptors allocated per attacking object in layer l,

W = number of attacking warheads.

For two layers, an $SSPk$ of 3/4 in the first layer and 1/2 in the second, eight attacking warheads, one shot per warhead in the first layer and five shots per surviving warhead in the second, the probability of no survivors is given by:

$$P_0(8) = (1 - [(1 - 0.75)^1 \cdot (1 - 0.5)^5])^8 = .939.$$

Figure 5.3—Calculating the Probability of No Survivors When the Effectiveness of Interceptors Differs Among Layers

As can be seen from Table 5.1, the least-cost solution (in bold) for this particular set of parameter values is to put four engagements per object in the first layer and three engagements per object in the second layer, for an expected total cost per object of 5.92.

Table 5.1

Worksheet for Determining the Least-Cost Defense Allocation

	1st Layer			2nd Layer		Total	Total Cost/
f	E/O	c	f	E/O	c	E/O	Object
1	10	1·10·1=10				10	10.0
1	8	1·8·1=8	0.1	1	0.1·2=0.20	9	8.20
1	6	1·6·1=6	0.18	2	0.18·2·2=0.72	8	6.72
1	**4**	**1·4·1=4**	**0.32**	**3**	**0.32·3·2=1.92**	**7**	**5.92**
1	2	1·2·1=2	0.56	4	0.56·4·2=4.48	6	6.48
			1	5	1·5·2=10	5	10.0

NOTE: $SSPk$ = 1/2 in first layer, 3/4 in second; $SSPl$ = 3/4 in first layer, not applicable in second; cost of one in first layer, two in second. Least-cost allocation in bold.

Section Summary

In this section we have showed how our methodology could be used to examine how differences in layer interceptor costs and buy-in costs affect the optimal allocation of resources.

- The impact of differences in interceptor costs among layers was similarly (and predictably) shown to affect the optimal allocation, with the allocation shifting toward more cost-effective layers.

- The effect of buy-in costs on the optimal allocation was also demonstrated. In our methodology, buy-in costs are amortized over attacking objects—buy-in costs may mitigate against investment unless there are sufficient numbers of attacking objects.

We also examined a case that involved simultaneous changes to several factors (including differences in per-interceptor costs). The next section examines how critical uncertainties arising from the "luck of the draw" might be taken into account in the development of an allocation "hedging" strategy.

6. Uncertainty

This section examines the sorts of uncertainties that can complicate missile defense planning, and provides the results of an illustrative Monte Carlo simulation-based analysis that addresses uncertainties regarding interceptor effectiveness and leakage rates.

Why Uncertainty Is Important

Concern about uncertainty stems from the possibility that we may not size our defenses correctly and thus could exhaust our supply of interceptors before the campaign is concluded.[1] There are a number of potential sources of uncertainty in planning missile defenses:

- the size of an attacker's inventory of missiles;

- the attacker's ability to launch large barrages that might saturate missile defenses;

- the level of warhead fractionation that might be achieved by the attacker's missile force, and the number of decoys that might be deployed;

- the nature of the measures the adversary might take to exploit missile defense system vulnerabilities;

- lack of knowledge about the effectiveness of interceptors (*SSPk*) and of kill assessment systems (*SSPl*); and

- the "luck of the draw" in processes that are inherently stochastic.

If we were able to buy and have ready for deployment in any individual campaign an unlimited supply of interceptors, there would be a sufficient stockpile to draw upon to hedge against unexpectedly bad effectiveness of interceptors or kill assessment systems in that campaign. Similarly, there would likely be an ample stockpile of interceptors to draw upon if the overall inventory was sized in anticipation of supporting a large number of campaigns, and the entire inventory of interceptors was deployed (or available) for any individual campaign.

---

[1]The authors wish to thank RAND colleague Rich Mesic for suggesting that we explicitly address uncertainty in this report.

Even if we knew the *SSPk* and *SSPl* and other factors, there are limitations in using expected values to determine the number of interceptors to deploy for a particular campaign. Expected values are only a surrogate for probabilistic distributions; the "luck of the draw" will affect the actual number of kills or the perceived number of leakers in a given defense layer, and could lead to a shortage of interceptors. We therefore need to hedge against "randomness": we must determine the inventory size that gives us a desired level of confidence that we will not run out of interceptors before the campaign is over.

The parametric expected-value approach documented in this report lends itself nicely to simulation techniques that can be used to examine the necessary inventory size to provide the desired confidence that the deployed system will achieve a high probability of zero leakers against a particular threat. We will next use Monte Carlo techniques to explore the variance about the expected values, and calculate the number of interceptors required to provide some level of probability (e.g., 90 percent) that in any particular campaign none of the layers will run out of interceptors.

Hedging Against Risk in Sizing the Inventory

Assume that we are facing the following hypothetical situation: we are confident from our intelligence that our defense will face no more than 64 attacking objects, none of which is capable of fractionation. Assume also the following:

- Operational testing and evaluation leads us to believe that the probability of kill for interceptors in all layers of a three-layer defense is 1/2.

- There is perfect kill assessment between layers one and two, but we have some uncertainties about the leakage rate from the second to third layers. This is because our kill assessment system, although deployed, has not been tested in an actual campaign. We assume that, on average, 1/2 of the objects killed in the second layer are likely to be misclassified as "not-killed" and shot at in the next layer. That is, the *SSPl* is 3/4 between the second and third layers.

Modeling Assumptions

We model the possible states that might be assumed by an attacking object as follows:

- We fix the defense firing doctrine at 1/2/7.[2]

- Each attacking object is thus allocated one interceptor in the first layer. This interceptor has a probability of kill of 1/2—whether a particular object is killed or not is determined by random draw.

- If the first layer does not *actually* kill the object, the second layer will fire two interceptors at the attacking object.

- If *either* interceptor in the second layer *actually* kills a particular object (determined by another draw) *and* there is a correct kill assessment for that kill (yet another draw), then the third layer will not fire any interceptors at that particular object. If neither interceptor kills the object, or if one or both kill the object but there is incorrect kill assessment, then seven interceptors will be fired against that particular object in the third layer.[3]

This logic dictates that if an object passes to the second layer, unless there is both a kill *and* a proper kill assessment, the third layer will see and fire at the object.

Simulation Results

We simulate 100 campaigns to determine the number of interceptors required to adhere to the firing doctrine of 1/2/7 while providing high confidence that we don't run out of interceptors, especially in the last layer. We do this by running a total of 6400 simulations of the possible outcomes for an individual object (64 objects per campaign, 100 campaigns) and then sequentially aggregating the results into groups of 64 objects to reflect the outcome of each of the 100 possible campaigns.

Results are reported in Table 6.1. The first three rows of the table report results for the individual layers, and the last row, "Total," is for the total number of interceptors used in each campaign. The expected number of interceptors allocated from our expected-value model is reported in the column titled "Expected Value," followed by the simulation results: the minimum and maximum numbers of interceptors required for each layer across the 100 campaigns, the mean number of interceptors, and the 90th percentiles for each

---

[2]The reader will recall that the firing doctrine 1/2/7 is the least-cost allocation for a three-layer system with the base case assumptions: *SSPk* of 1/2 for each layer, *SSPl* of 1/2 for all layers, equal cost per interceptor in each layer, yielding >90 percent probability of total threat negation. We are using this firing doctrine rather than the actual least-cost allocation of 2/2/6 both to simplify comparisons with the base case and to examine the robustness of the base case architecture in the face of poorer kill assessment than expected.

[3]Thus, for each kill in the second layer, there is a separate kill assessment (e.g., if a particular object is "killed" twice (by draw), then two kill assessments (draws) are made).

Table 6.1

Required Interceptors from Monte Carlo Simulation

	Expected Value	Minima	Maxima	Mean	90th Percentile
Layer 1	64	64	64	64	64 (1.0)
Layer 2	64	48	90	64	72 (1.1)
Layer 3	126	70	189	122	154 (1.2)
Total	254	184	343	250	286 (1.1)
	[3.97]				[4.47]

NOTES: Expected *SSPk* in each layer is 1/2; *SSPl* = 3/4 between second and third layer. Numbers in parentheses () are ratio of 90th percentile to expected value. Numbers in square brackets [] are ratios of total engagements to initial attacking objects. Numbers may not total because results reflect separate runs.

layer and for the total interceptors used. The numbers in parentheses following the 90th percentiles are the ratio of the 90th percentile to the expected value, a rough index of the effect of uncertainty on inventory size.

As is clear from the differences between the columns for the 90th percentile and for the expected-value optimal allocation of 1/2/7, the simulation results suggest that if we were to use the optimal 254 interceptors from the expected-value model, we would run short of interceptors in a good number of the campaigns, 43 out of 100 in our simulation—a 43 percent chance of catastrophic failure. Shortfalls occurred in the second layer in 44 of the campaigns, and in 46 campaigns the third layer ran short.[4] If we want to provide high confidence that in a given campaign there is 90 percent confidence we will not run out of interceptors, then we should plan to deploy about 286 interceptors, with most of the additional interceptors going into the third layer.[5] Compared with the allocation for the base case, the reader can see that the demand to hedge against uncertainty (the "luck of the draw") can significantly increase the required size of the inventory, especially in the last layers.

---

[4]We used the binomial distribution to confirm the reasonableness of the simulated 90th percentile for the second layer by computing the cumulative probability of all possible numbers of leakers, from 0 through 64. Since two interceptors would be fired at each object surviving to the second layer, the 90th percentile value of 72 for the second layer in the table would mean that, on average, 36 objects survived from the first layer. The binomial distribution revealed that the 90th percentile in fact occurs between 36 (cumulative probability of 0.870) and 37 (cumulative probability of 0.916).

[5]As might be expected, the effect of uncertainty compounds from layer to layer.

Section Summary

In this section we used Monte Carlo simulation techniques to examine the effect of the "luck of the draw," and we constructed a hedging strategy that would provide a high level of confidence that we would have enough interceptors to ensure 90 percent confidence of no exhaustion in a particular campaign. This required inventory was substantially larger than that suggested by the expected-value model, and it was allocated far more heavily to the last layer.

There are obviously many other issues related to uncertainty, including the impact of correlated errors in kill assessment on large salvos, *a priori* measurement of effectiveness, operational issues relating to robustness of a missile defense system that is deployed into a theater over time, and how the architecture or firing doctrine might be adapted over the course of a campaign to mitigate particular technical or doctrinal problems. All these issues are worthy of serious research; our purpose, however, was to show how the methodology can be extended to assist in the analysis of many such issues, not to do the analysis.

The next section shows how the methodology might used to support an illustrative "mission area analysis" for the mission area of theater missile defense.

7. An Illustrative Mission Area Analysis

This section briefly introduces some broader programmatic issues and then provides an illustrative "mission area analysis" or COEA (cost and operational effectiveness analysis) for theater missile defense that suggests a framework for comparing different programmatic options in terms of their level of effectiveness, marginal costs, and buy-in costs.

Ingredients of a Mission Area Analysis

The essential ingredients of a mission area analysis include statements about the following:

- The mission area—countering theater ballistic missiles equipped with weapons of mass destruction (WMD).
- The context—major crisis or conflict in some theater where U.S. vital interests are at stake.
- The threat—the number and type of attacking missiles.
- The countering players—midcourse/terminal defenses, boost/postboost defenses, counterforce operations, passive defenses.
- The measure of outcome—in our example, the probability of no leakers.
- The optimum allocation of resources among the players—to be calculated.
- The total resources required to counter various threats—to be calculated.

The Threat and Measure of Outcome

Consider a threat of 51 missiles containing around ten submunitions each for a total of 512 submunitions,[1] and a requirement for greater than 90 percent probability that no operational weapons impact on friendly soil.

---

[1]Because powers of two simplify our computations, we will (with negligible loss of exactness) round the number of submunitions from 510 to 512.

The Countering Players

The following systems are available for consideration:

- Deployment of midcourse and terminal systems has just commenced, and all development and engineering costs for these systems are already sunk. The cost of deploying these systems is $7 million for each engagement. The "probability of kill" (*SSPk*), given an engagement, for these systems is 1/2, while the "probability of leaking" (*SSPl*) from the midcourse to terminal layer is 3/4.

- There exists an option for deploying a better surveillance system for performing kill assessment. This system will reportedly reduce the *SSPl* after a midcourse engagement from 3/4 to 1/2 (that is, it will provide perfect kill assessment). There are still development and engineering costs ahead, however, as well as the cost of manufacturing and then deploying this enhanced system.

- There also exists an option for developing and deploying a system that will attack missiles before fractionation (during boost and postboost phases and before submunitions separate),[2] but there remain significant development, engineering, manufacturing, and deployment costs for this system.

Programmatic Options

Option One

The first option is to deploy a two-layer (midcourse and terminal) system to handle the entirety of the threat—but no improved kill assessment system, and no boost/postboost systems.

Given that there are 512 objects, and given an *SSPk* of 1/2, we know by the "rule of four" that we must have 13 engagements per surviving object to attain over 90 percent probability of no survivors.

Figure 7.1 shows the cost implications of various partitions of these 13 engagements into first- and second-layer allocations. The cost per attacking object for the endpoints is 13, since all are allocated to the second layer (abscissa = 0) or all to the first layer (abscissa = 13). Between these points, the cost per attacking object falls to its minimum (about 6.85) at four engagements

---

[2]There are a number of possible operational concepts for destroying missiles during these phases.

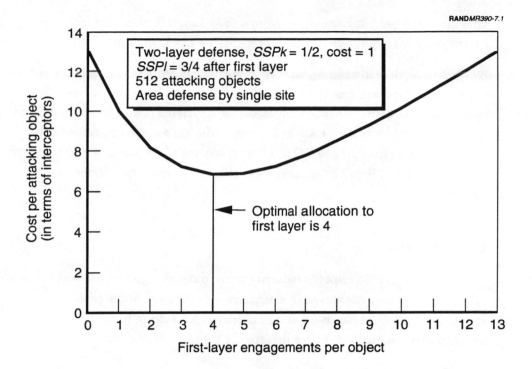

Figure 7.1—Option One: Cost Implications of Alternative Firing Doctrines

per object in the midcourse layer and nine in the terminal layer, a firing doctrine of 4/9.[3] If we assume that interceptors in each layer cost $7 million each, then the total cost in dollars for 512 attacking objects is approximately $24.6 billion (512 · 6.85 · $7 million).

Option Two

The second option would be to add a kill assessment system that changes the *SSPl* from 3/4 to 1/2, that is, provides perfect kill assessment between the first and second layer. The presence of this system will reduce the costs of deploying the midcourse and terminal defenses required to counter the threat of 512 objects.

The optimal allocation for 13 total engagements per surviving object in this case is the firing doctrine 3/10, and the total cost per attacking object is now 4.25.[4] Thus, deploying an improved kill assessment system reduces the cost (in terms of

---

[3]Here, $6.85 = 4 \cdot (3/4)^4$. The function being graphed is $x + (n - x)SSPl^x$, where n is the total number of engagements per object demanded for the defense system (13 in this case), x is the number of engagements per object in the first layer, and $(n - x)$ is the number of engagements per object in the second layer.

[4]This can be determined analytically or graphically, as above.

engagements) per attacking object from 6.85 to 4.25. The total cost for interceptors in option two is $15.2 billion (512 · 4.25 · $7 million).

By deploying the kill assessment system we have saved $9.4 billion in the cost of deploying midcourse and terminal systems. To do so, however, we incur the cost of deploying the enhanced kill assessment system.[5] Thus, one boundary of the cost-effectiveness domain is as follows: *if* the kill assessment system can change the *SSPl* from 3/4 to 1/2 at a cost of less than $9.4 billion, then the system can be justified. Table 7.1 summarizes the two programmatic options just described.

Option Three

We now address a concept for reducing the number of objects presented to the midcourse/terminal defenses. We can derive a boundary in the cost-effectiveness domain based upon the cost savings resulting from boost/postboost phase defenses that reduce the number of objects

Table 7.1

Summary of Programmatic Options

Option	Description
Midcourse/terminal defenses	
First layer	$SSPk = 1/2$, $SSPl = 3/4$
Second layer	$SSPk = 1/2$, $SSPl$ is N/A
Optimal firing doctrine	4/9
Cost per attacking object	6.85 engagements per object
Total defense costs	$24.6 billion
Add kill assessment system	
First layer	$SSPk = 1/2$, $SSPl = 1/2$
Second layer	$SSPk = 1/2$, $SSPl$ is N/A
Optimal firing doctrine	3/10
Cost per attacking object	4.25 engagements per object
Total defense costs	$15.2 billion
Maximum cost for kill assessment	
system	$9.4 billion
Net savings	$4.4 billion

---

[5]This conclusion is based upon the size of the threat (512 attacking objects); for far fewer attackers, the system might not be justified.

the midcourse/terminal defenses must engage, thereby reducing the costs of these layers.[6]

The first step is to define the function of "cost" versus "effectiveness" for the prefractionation system(s). Suppose that, based upon research, we believe that the relationship between the number of units deployed and the fraction of missiles killed is captured by the expression

$$\text{fraction killed} = 1 - e^{-n/x}$$

where n is the number of defense units deployed and x is a scaling factor, assumed to be 10. Figure 7.2 plots the function with various values of n;[7] note that the function exhibits diminishing returns to additional levels of effort, as would be expected.

Suppose we determined through modeling and simulation that with ten units of a boost/postboost defense (i.e., $n = 10$) we could, over the course of the

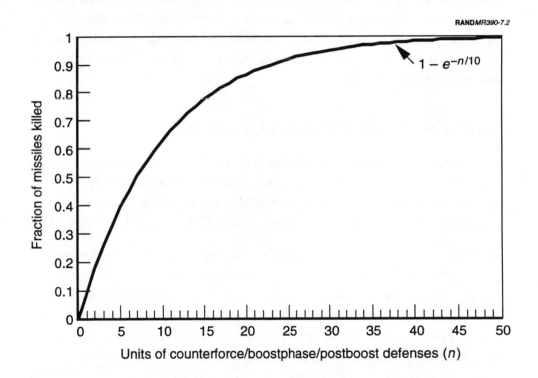

Figure 7.2—Level of Effort of Prefractionation and Percent of Attacker's Missiles Killed

---

[6]Although we have little evidence regarding either "cost" or "effectiveness" of systems in each layer, in order to illustrate a possible approach to a "cost-effectiveness" analysis, we will continue with some notional numbers.

[7]A similar functional form with different parameters might be established for counterforce.

campaign, kill 63 percent of the 51 attacking objects. With $n = 10$, $x = 10$, and the resulting value of our function equal to 63 percent, we may now estimate the fraction of attacking objects that are killed by fixing x at 10 and varying the number of units of boost/postboost defenses (n). Assume finally that a separate cost analysis indicates that the buy-in cost for boost/postboost defenses is $3 billion and the production cost of each unit is $500 million. Table 7.2 reports the cost consequences of deploying various numbers of units of prefractionation defenses.

In option three the optimal allocation is to deploy 16 units of a prefractionation system for boost-phase and postboost-phase defenses. This will provide the capability to kill around 80 percent of the 51 attacking missiles before they fractionate, and the total cost will be reduced from $24.6 to $15.3 billion, for a net savings of $9.3 billion.

Note that in determining the above costs, we did not consider the costs associated with proliferating terminal defenses to provide coverage for a large area. A surveillance system that allows early commitment of terminal interceptors would provide a larger footprint and thus reduce the number (and cost) of terminal sites needed. This is, therefore, another tradeoff to examine in a full-fledged mission area analysis.

Representing the Tradeoff Graphically

We can now construct a "cost-effectiveness domain" by plotting two functions—the dollars avoided on midcourse/terminal defenses as a function of the effectiveness of the boost/postboost defenses, and the dollars spent on prefractionation defenses. This is done in Figure 7.3.

In the figure, the large region between the two curves is the "cost-effectiveness domain," where it is efficient to buy prefractionation defenses. The maximum savings occurs where the slopes of the two curves are identical. Now compare this with the $24.6 billion for the two-layer midcourse/terminal system alone and note the savings of $9.3 (24.6 − 11.0 − 4.3) billion. Note also that the buy-in cost does not affect the optimum number of units to buy to gain maximum savings but does, of course, decrement this savings—dollar for dollar.

Section Summary

The reader can see that there are innumerable variants of the analyses one can do to compare different programmatic options, but we believe we have achieved the

Table 7.2

Tradeoffs Between Prefractionation Defenses and Midcourse/Terminal Defenses

Units of Prefraction- ation Defenses	Percent Boosters Killed	Attack Objects Presented to Midcourse/ Terminal Defenses	Number of Engagements/ Surviv. Object	Optimal Firing Doctrine	Number of Engagements/ Attack Object	Cost of M/T Defenses	Cost of Prefraction. Defenses ($B)	Total Cost ($B)	Net Savings ($B)
0	0	512	13	4/9	6.85	24.6	0	24.6	0
2	18.1	419	12	4/8	6.53	19.2	4.0	23.2	1.4
4	33.0	343	12	4/8	6.53	15.7	5.0	20.7	3.9
6	45.1	281	12	4/8	6.53	12.8	6.0	18.8	5.8
8	55.1	230	12	4/8	6.53	10.5	7.0	17.5	7.1
10	63.2	188	11	4/7	6.21	8.2	8.0	16.2	8.4
12	69.9	154	11	4/7	6.21	6.7	9.0	15.7	8.9
14	75.3	126	11	4/7	6.21	5.5	10.0	15.5	9.1
16	**79.8**	**103**	**10**	**4/6**	**5.90**	**4.3**	**11.0**	**15.3**	**9.3**
18	83.5	85	10	4/6	5.90	3.5	12.0	15.5	9.1
20	86.5	69	10	4/6	5.90	2.8	13.0	15.8	8.8

Note: Optimal buy of prefractionation defenses in bold. For derivation of "engagements per surviving object," see Table 2.6.

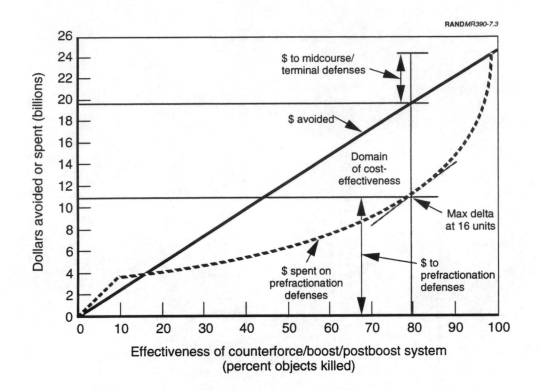

Figure 7.3—Cost-Effectiveness Domain

objective of demonstrating how the methodology might provide the analytic underpinning for a mission area analysis (or, if you prefer, mission area COEA) and a road map for the "players" in this mission area of theater missile defense. The next section provides concluding remarks.

8. Concluding Remarks

Throughout this report, our aims have been twofold: to describe a simple methodology for determining how to allocate resources among layers of a multilayered missile defense, and to provide illustrative results both to show that the methodology offers a simple-yet-robust approach to analysis in this mission area and to provide critical insights into understanding where the leverage exists. Our discussion of the methodology began simply and became successively more sophisticated:

- We began by showing the logic of allocating resources among layers of a missile defense system by using a simple worksheet-based approach.

- We described more formally a simple model that relied on only four parameters—the number of layers in the missile defense, the number of attacking objects, the demanded probability of no survivors, and the $SSPk$ of interceptors in each layer—to determine the optimal firing doctrine to provide the desired level of confidence of no survivors of an attacking force while minimizing the number of interceptors required to achieve that confidence.

- We then expanded the model to take into account several other operational parameters (i.e., the quality of kill assessment, fractionation, saturation and exhaustion, and multiple sites to provide a "footprint") and cost variations (i.e., different interceptor costs among layers and buy-in costs). We were then able to demonstrate, in a first-order way, exactly how these parameters affect the optimal allocation. Taking into account these additional parameters did not add undue complexity to the basic model.

- We then examined the effect of some critical uncertainties on the size of the missile defense system required to provide a demanded level of confidence of no survivors over the campaign without exhausting the inventory of interceptors.

- Finally, we provided an illustrative mission area analysis to show how our model might be used in assessing broad programmatic tradeoffs within a mission area.

While there are many policy-relevant insights offered in the course of this study, we will close by emphasizing three:

- There are numerous and substantial benefits inherent in architectures that rely on multiple layers of missile defense. Notably, they achieve high levels of effectiveness at far lower cost than that of a single-layer defense.

- Nevertheless, the costs associated with missile defenses—layered or not—are likely to be substantial. As an illustration, we examined an optimized three-layered defense made up of interceptors with an *SSPk* of 1/2 and 64 attacking objects. The optimum firing doctrine of this defense was one engagement per attacking object in the first layer, two in the second, and seven in the third. This generates a requirement for 184 interceptors to enforce a greater than 90 percent probability of zero leakers. Said another way, we must deploy 2.875 interceptors for every object in the attacker's inventory. If we want to hedge against exhausting our interceptors in any particular campaign, the cost is even higher. Nevertheless, if only a single layer of defenses is fielded, the attendant cost of 640 interceptors remains far higher.

- Finally, there is high leverage in engaging attacking objects at the earliest possible stage, and certainly before fractionation (preboost, boost, and postboost phases). There are other effects we did not examine (e.g., the effects of correlated errors in kill assessment) that would also argue for early intercept before fractionation.

Our purpose has not been to provide a comprehensive analysis but rather to introduce a methodolology and show how it can be easily extended to consider more complex planning considerations. Accordingly, we did not provide a definitive and comprehensive analysis of all the technical and operational issues and sensitivity analyses attendant to planning missile defenses. We leave it to others to apply or adapt the methodology and to examine cases beyond those reported here.

In closing, it is the authors' hope that the methodology developed here is found to be useful to both planners and policymakers in assessing the broad programmatic options available for providing effective missile defenses.

Appendix
Base Case and Excursions

Table A.1 summarizes the base case and the various excursions that were
described in Sections 3 through 5 of this report, in terms of the parameter values,
optimal firing doctrine and allocation of interceptors to each layer, cost per
attacker's inventory object, and probability of no survivors of an attacking force.

Table A.1

Summary of Cases

Case	Case Description	Layer	SSP*k*	SSP*l*	Fractionation	Footprint	Cost	Firing Doctrine	Allocation	Ratio Cost/ Missile	Probability of Zero Leakers
A	Base case	1	1/2	1/2	1	1	1	1	64		
		2	1/2	1/2	1	1	1	2	64		
		3	1/2	—	1	1	1	7	56		
								10	184	2.875	.939
B	One-layer system	1	—	—	—	—	—	0	0		
		2	—	—	—	—	—	0	0		
		3	1/2	—	1	1	1	10	640		
								10	640	10.0	.939
C	Higher SSP*k* in first layer	1	3/4	1/4	1	1	1	1	64		
		2	1/2	1/2	1	1	1	2	32		
		3	1/2	—	1	1	1	6	24		
								9	120	1.875	.939
D	Lower SSP*k* in first layer	1	1/4	3/4	1	1	1	1	64		
		2	1/2	1/2	1	1	1	2	96		
		3	1/2	—	1	1	1	7	84		
								10	244	3.8125	.910
E	Higher SSP*l* after second layer	1	1/2	1/2	1	1	1	2	128		
		2	1/2	3/4	1	1	1	2	32		
		3	1/2	—	1	1	1	6	54		
								10	214	3.3438	.939

Table A.1—continued

Case	Case Description	Layer	SSPk	SSPl	Fractionation	Footprint	Cost	Firing Doctrine	Allocation	Ratio Cost/Missile	Probability of Zero Leakers
F	Fractionation	1	1/2	1/2	1	1	1	6	384		
		2	1/2	1/2	16	1	1	2	32		
		3	1/2	—	—	1	1	6	24		
								—	440	6.875	.939
G	Eight sites for "footprint"	1	1/2	1/2	1	1	1	2	128		
		2	1/2	1/2	1	1	1	5	80		
		3	1/2	—	1	3	1	3	12		
								10	220	3.438	.939
H	Higher cost in first layer	1	1/2	1/2	1	1	2	0	0		
		2	1/2	1/2	1	1	1	3	192		
		3	1/2	—	1	1	1	7	56		
								10	248	3.875	.939
I	Lower cost in first layer	1	1/2	1/2	1	1	1/2	2	128		
		2	1/2	1/2	1	1	1	2	32		
		3	1/2	—	1	1	1	6	24		
								10	184	1.875	.939
J	Multiple changes, two layers	1	—	—	—	—	—	—	—		
		2	1/2	3/4	1	1	1	4	256		
		3	3/4	1/4	1	1	2	3	61		
								7	317	5.898	.939